RIVERWATCH

RIVERWATCH

The waterside diaries of a naturalist-angler

MARK EVERARD

HOBNOB PRESS

First published in the United Kingdom in 2018

by The Hobnob Press,
8 Lock Warehouse, Severn Road, Gloucester GL1 2GA
www.hobnobpress.co.uk

British Library Cataloguing in Publication Data
A catalogue record for this book is available from the British Library

ISBN 978-1-906978-57-0

Typeset in Doves Type.
Typesetting and origination by John Chandler

Printed by Lightning Source

CONTENTS

About the Author

Introduction to Riverwatch   1

APRIL   3

     Cuckoo flower time   5

     Kissing frogs   7

     The mammalian circus   9

     The wisdom of trees   12

     March of the killer lobsters   14

MAY   17

     Dance of the 'boingy-boingy flies'   19

     The white month   22

     Dandelion clocks   24

     A healthy riverside walk   27

     A riot of grasses   29

JUNE   31

     Walking on water   33

     Halycon days   35

     Chubby river   38

     Rivers of peace   40

     Snow in summer   43

JULY   45

     Fragments of wilderness   47

     The serpent in our landscape   49

     Chemical warfare by the riverside   52

Fifty shades of brown 54
Nature's ecological economy 56
AUGUST 59
The water snake 61
The horse stinger 63
Whose river? 65
What's the point of wasps? 68
Feast and famine 70
SEPTEMBER 73
A proliferation of fishes 75
Sleeping in the river mud 77
Common willows 80
Jewels in the landscape 83
Water babies 86
OCTOBER 89
Falling leaves 91
Busy bees 93
Sounds of the seasons 96
Floodplain forays 98
Pearl-laden cobwebs 100
NOVEMBER 103
Muddying the water 105
More hens! 107
Who doesn't love worms? 109
The riparian pharmacopoeia 112
The season of the plover 114
DECEMBER 117
Red-breasted companions 119
December moths 121

Where the wild things are   123

Mobile homes in the silt   125

Flying kittens   127

JANUARY   129

Crusty creatures   131

Both sides now   134

The 'Jenny Wren'   136

Seasons gone wild   139

Spare the dredger!   142

FEBRUARY   145

Gridirons   147

What's a fish?   150

Return of the otter   152

Humble bees   155

The nature of nature   157

MARCH   159

March magic!   161

Low-flying mice   163

The Mundella legacy   165

Here be pterodactyls!   167

Turn! Turn! Turn!   169

ABOUT THE AUTHOR

D<small>R</small> M<small>ARK</small> E<small>VERARD</small> is passionate about rivers, the living things within them, and the many benefits that they confer upon us.

Mark completed his BSc (first class) in Freshwater and Marine Biology followed by a PhD studying aspects of pollution in freshwater ecosystems, and has both lived and worked with water ever since. His studies and development work have taken him to all five major continents, including considerable time spent on water management in developing countries where a little expertise on water in the landscape can protect ecosystems and thereby improve people's lives.

Mark is the author of many books – 24 of them at the time of writing – addressing aspects of ecosystems, fish in particular, as well as more widely on sustainable development. Mark is also a frequent contributor to television (BBC *Springwatch* amongst others) and radio, and author of many scientific journal, technical and popular press articles.

But all this is rather dry detail!

Above all, Mark is passionate about the water itself and the myriad living things within and around it, as well as the many ways they support our wellbeing in biophysical, cultural and many other ways. This includes angling – Mark is a keen angler and a prominent face in angling media – which is a fine excuse to remain still by a river whilst all manner of everyday miracles reveal themselves!

Riverwatch began life as series of regular articles in the local magazine *Signpost*, distributed free to households in six villages in north Wiltshire around which the upper Bristol Avon runs. Modifications of many of these articles formed initial input to this book, before the writing process took on a life of its own.

Above all, Mark is a communicator about the wonders of the natural world, hoping to enthuse others about how fantastic but above all important this awareness is for both its and our conjoined wellbeing.

INTRODUCTION TO
Riverwatch

W E ARE RIVER creatures.
In purely biological terms, water comprises around a third of our body mass and we need to replenish roughly two-and-a-half to four litres of it every day, and sometimes more than that.

Rivers are also a fundamental force shaping the landscapes we inhabit, find food, and with which we co-evolved. Water flows gorge ravines in uplands, throw serpentine meanders into lowlands, sculpt floodplains and form broad estuaries as they merge into coastal seas. These flows and forms in turn comprise key elements of aesthetically, spiritually, economically and culturally important geographical settings, many of our settlements taking riverine names such as -bourne, -mouth, -ford, -ham, -port and -bridge.

We harvest fish, plants, invertebrates and other food from river waters, which also moisten and drain the soils we depend upon for much of our sustenance.

So profound is our relationship with rivers that every culture has deities, ceremonies or legends associated with flowing water, many encoding important messages about its value and associated wise stewardship practices.

But *Riverwatch* is about a great deal in addition to the philosophy of water. It is above all a celebration of river life. The book comprises vignettes of the wildlife of rivers as it unfolds before and around us month by month. These observations and insights are gleaned from a lifetime in thrall to rivers. I have worked and angled on so many of them across the globe, but *Riverwatch* relates to observations and thoughts from many years spent as a naturalist and fisherman alongside Britain's diverse running fresh waters.

So much enrichment can flow from spending idle time by moving water. In this context, I interpret idleness as an active term, as activity is required to hold at bay the strident clamour for attention endemic to contemporary lifestyles and pervasive media. In so doing, we allow ourselves valuable moments of immersion in the unfolding wonders of river life as it morphs with the turn of the seasons. Such a state of reflective idleness is most readily achieved with the excuse of a fishing rod in hand, or perhaps a camera, drawing pad or other quiet pursuit offering sanctuary from life's rowdy demands.

Riverwatch is, as the book's sub-title elaborates, the waterside diaries (and also sketchpad) of a naturalist-angler keen to share some of many rich experiences of the daily miracles of river life.

The book kicks off with the burst of springtime life that we experience in April, running month-by-month throughout the full calendar year as seasons wax and wane giving way to successive fresh instalments of wildlife drama, but pausing a while for some deeper musings *en route*.

This book is to be dipped into and enjoyed. I have been sparing in the inclusion of Latin names for species so that those inquisitive enough to seek out more information have leads to follow. However, as my intent is to offer far more than a dry, learned monograph, I hope that your eye can skip over these bracketed terms without disrupting your reading and enjoyment. Who knows, perhaps you may derive a little inspiration from reading *Riverwatch* to encourage you out to the moist riverbank to immerse yourself in the enriching kaleidoscope of riverside nature as its constancy is enacted through perpetual change by the turn of the seasons.

APRIL

CUCKOO FLOWER TIME

DAYS ARE LENGTHENING; nights perceptibly less cool. We may soon see the first Sand Martins (*Riparia riparia*), House Martins (*Delichon urbicum*) and Swallows (*Hirundo rustica*), and hear the first call of various warblers secreted in vegetation. Frogs have already deposited their globular masses of spawn, newts and Pond Skaters returning to the water from their insulated hibernation sites.

But the weather flatters to deceive at this time of year. One minute there is a bright sky that ushers the vanessids – Small Tortoiseshell, Peacock and Comma butterflies – out of torpor as over-wintering adult butterflies. The next sees squalls of icy rain. Is it spring just because we have passed its nominal 'first day': the equinox in the third week of March? The leaf buds of the May bush may be greening and fit to burst, but the froth of Blackthorn blossom in the hedges tells a different tale of a prolonged 'Blackthorn Winter'.

Whilst we may be deceived, nature always knows the true story coded in strong and more subtle signals of climate, day length, prevailing winds, temperature and moisture. But, if there is one sure signal that nature knows when spring is truly springing, it is the emergence of delicate lilac-pink blossoms of the Cuckoo Flower enlivening wet meadows.

The Cuckoo Flower (*Cardamine pratensis*) goes by many local names: 'Milkmaids', 'Lady's Smock' and many more besides that convey the delicacy and timing of this short perennial plant, sending up shoots early in the year from rhizomes and overwintered seeds to paint the spring meadow with delicate blossoms then drying back with its pods of fertile seeds before the sward is swamped by the late spring surge of taller, more robust grasses and herbs. As a crucifer (family Cruciferae), there are four equal petals to each flower, several arranged in a head raised above the still low sward.

The name 'Cuckoo Flower' narrates the timing of the flower's opening. The bird, like the flower appropriating its name, is most readily observed in river valleys, a long-tailed, brownish species a little bigger than a blackbird occasionally seen plying the open space of the floodplain from treeline to treeline. The characteristic call of the male Common Cuckoo (*Cuculus canorus*), announcing his presence and calling for mates on migratory return to our shores from the Sahel, was commonplace when I was a child. Regrettably it is now far less frequently heard, the 'common' epithet at odds with the bird's sharp population decline and subsequent inclusion on the IUCN's Red List of endangered species.

The Cuckoo Flower too has declined with the progressive loss of wetlands across the landscape, though remains relatively common where floodplains are better connected to rivers, on flushes on hill slopes and across low-lying land where moisture accumulates.

Infusions of Cuckoo Flower leaves have been used to treat indigestion and promote appetite, and the fresh leaves and flowers have formerly been imbued with antirheumatic, antiscorbutic, antispasmodic, carminative, digestive, diuretic and various other properties and used to treat skin complaints, asthma and hysteria. Leaves and young shoots are also edible, either raw or cooked, and reputedly rich in minerals and vitamins (especially vitamin C) though with a bitter and pungent cress-like taste (unsurprisingly for a plant in the same family as Watercress and various brassicas). The Cuckoo Flower is also the county flower of both Cheshire and Brecknockshire. It is also a food plant, along with several other crucifer species, of the Orange-tip butterfly (*Anthocharis cardamines*) that is also on the wing this season.

Whatever its other attributes, the Cuckoo Flower for me is the colour and harbinger of spring, affirming that the seasons' wheel is turning, and a welcome, delicately hued addition to the palette of the river valley.

KISSING FROGS

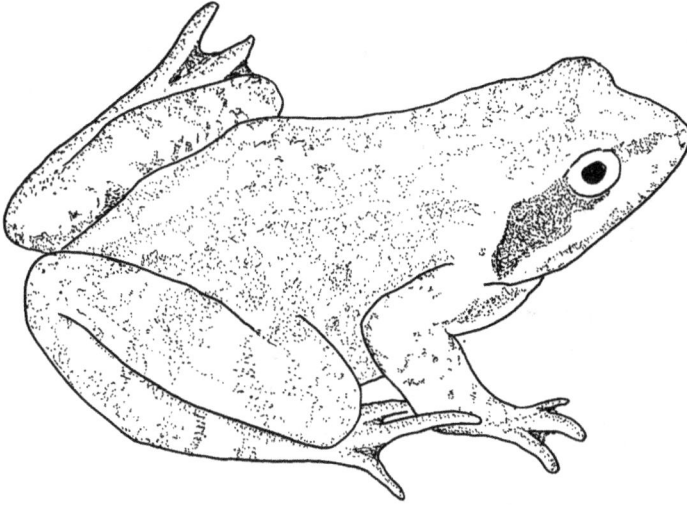

Frogs are as much a symbol of spring as Easter bunnies, daffodils and 'lamb's tails', whether these tails happen to be on willow bushes or lambs themselves. Kids and adults alike (mainly) love frogs, with their bulbous eyes and the baritone croaks of breeding males advertising their presence as they return to ponds to breed as winter loosens its hold. Although frogs do not always fare well in flowing waters and particularly those with strong populations of fish and other predators of their tadpoles, the many pools and wetlands naturally forming part of river valleys are distinct strongholds.

Frogs also have a familiar but no less miraculous life cycle, masses of jelly-wrapped eggs hatching into tadpoles, initially with external gills and no legs but metamorphosing over a period of four or five months into perfect miniature 'froglets' that subsequently hop off into moist undergrowth and other hidey-holes to live out an adult life feeding mainly on small soft-bodied invertebrates. Britain's frogs typically take three or four years to mature to breeding age, and can live for ten to twenty years in captivity though are subject to such a degree of predation that these venerable ages are highly unlikely in the wild.

Over much of Great Britain, we find just a single species: the Common Frog (*Rana temporaria*). However, the Pool Frog (*Pelophylax lessonae*) may once have been native to Norfolk, and has since been reintroduced from continental Europe into southern England. The Marsh Frog (*Pelophylax ridibundus*) and Edible Frog (*Pelophylax esculentus*) have also since been reintroduced from across the Channel. The American Bullfrog (*Rana catesbeiana*) has also bred in the UK as an accidental introduction. Some 4,740 species of frog occur around the world, though 120 have gone extinct since 1980.

The Common Frog is, alas, far less common today. Globally, including at home, a fungal plague is devastating frog populations. Add to this massive loss of suitable habitat: 65% of the UK's small ponds were lost largely due to agricultural intensification during the Twentieth Century, exacerbated by increasing urban sprawl and associated infrastructure. Furthermore, fish ponds are generally not favourable habitat as fish, as well as herons, foxes, badgers and various other bird and mammal carnivores (as well as invertebrates and other pond wildlife), are amongst the major predators of frogs and tadpoles. In fact, ideal habitat for frogs, as indeed for many of our amphibians, is provided by temporary pools which wet up in winter and spring but then dry out in the summer ensuring that potential predatory fish are unable to establish. In the light of this scale of environmental change, it is increasingly hard for frogs to maintain viable populations, and to spread between ever more fragmented pools.

These factors reinforce the importance of suitable garden ponds as substitute habitat, which can be critical to the viability of frog populations in some areas. We can all do our bit to encourage them, and to enjoy their continued presence in our lives.

Interestingly, we know that frogs go "*Ribbit Ribbit*"... only they mainly don't! Some species near Hollywood do and, since their calls have featured in so many film sound tracks, there is a misplaced assumption that this is a more general frog call. In fact, the call of our native Common Frog is limited only to breeding males in early spring, and sounds more like a farty croak than anything!

THE MAMMALIAN CIRCUS

T HE RETURN OF the Otter (the Eurasian Otter, *Lutra lutra*) to many British rivers is a topic to which we will return later in *Riverwatch* as it is a 'good news' story resulting from the progressive removal of various dangerous pollutants from our landscape, albeit that the Otter's return is not universally welcomed by all sectors of society and particularly those with vested interests in overstocked fisheries. However, this resurgence of Otters is just part of a wider shift in the aquatic mammalian fauna of our river valleys over the past quarter century and more.

Up to the very early 1990s, the Water Vole (*Arvicola terrestris*) – 'Ratty' of 'Wind in the Willows' fame but in reality very much distinct from a rat – was still a common sight paddling across or munching vegetation in the margins of my home river in Wiltshire, though more generally was already a species in precipitous decline. This short-sighted, charming little chunky herbivore was once ubiquitous across lowland Britain's pondscapes and streams, and also a familiar sound as it chewed noisily on vegetation or dived into the water with a distinctive 'plop' when alarmed. Alas, no more.

American Mink (*Mustela vison*) escaped from British fur farms, and were first confirmed as breeding in the wild here in 1956. By 1967, Mink were present in over half the counties of England and Wales. Further waves of farm escapes, famously including one in my home village Great Somerford, were to follow. This voracious predator is generally, but not exclusively, associated with the waterside. Mink are inefficient hunters of fish, mainly preying opportunistically on bankside mammals, birds, crayfish and amphibians, but also known to raid chicken coops. But also, unlike any native British mammal, Mink are agile and lithe enough to access the once secure bankside burrows of the Water Vole. And therein lies the primary cause of the Water Vole's catastrophic decline following the establishment of strong local Mink populations, and their still ongoing spread across the British Isles.

The return of the Otter adds an interesting twist to this tale in recent years. Otters and Mink belong to the same family (*Mustelidae*: carnivorous mammals also including badgers, weasels and martens), and are also highly territorial. There is evidence that Mink fare considerably less well when Otters repopulate a catchment, as Otters are far bigger and also distinctly intolerant of their American cousins. So there is a chink of light – perhaps no more than that – for the few relic populations of Water Voles still persisting across British rivers.

Another positive adaptation is that Water Voles are highly fecund, producing three or even four litters of up to six young during a typical year. Much like the Kingfisher, this allows for rapid recolonisation after the ravages of severe winters, flooding during the breeding season or other crises. In years when Mink have been all but absent, I have seen Water Voles spreading from populated areas. However, these 'breakout' populations rapidly succumb once Mink reappear.

Another chink of light is seen in the behaviour of the Water Vole in continental Europe. 'Our' Water Voles were once named *Arvicola amphibius*, recognising their aquatic association, but this same species is mainly terrestrial in habit across the channel (hence harmonisation of the Latin name to *Arvicola terrestris*).

The decline of once pervasive water bodies and wetlands in the landscape – a progressive decrease in ponds, marshes, streams and their unmanaged margins as well as open ditches – imposes further substantial pressures on Water Vole populations, denying them refuge across river valleys from which to rebuild predated populations. Such connected networks of wetlands, apparently so insignificant in isolation, are in reality of huge importance for the functioning of the countryside not merely ecologically but in terms of their roles in regulating hydrology and so buffering the effects of both flood and drought.

Science is emerging that Water Voles and American Mink can co-exist where a suitable matrix of off-channel wet refuges is still intact across the landscape. This is certainly the case in continental Europe, where Water Voles cohabit landscapes perfectly well with the admittedly rather different, and now endangered, European Mink (*Mustela lutreola*). So better valuation and measures to safeguard or, ideally, restore our wetland heritage, with all of the many wider co-benefits it provides, may just offer a route back for the imperilled but always charming Water Vole – dear old Ratty – that was once such an omnipresent part of our waterside experiences.

THE WISDOM OF TREES

YOU MAY OR may not be familiar with the old saying, pertinent at this time of year, that "*If the oak is out before the ash, then we'll only have a splash. But if the ash is out before the oak, then we'll surely have a soak*". Like many long-established country sayings, there is wisdom hidden in the rhyme. The leaves of the oak unfurled first in 2017 and also in 2018 in the part of Wiltshire in which I live and, despite a great deal of rain in the preceding months, the rhyme held true with a dry summer to follow. As a generality, the old saying has not been too far wrong in my experience.

Country people will also be familiar with the phenomenon of the 'Blackthorn Winter'. When the froth of blackthorn blossoms paints the hedgerows as March segues through into April, we can expect biting winds and prolonged cold until the blossoms fade and fall.

And then we have the saying "*Ne'er cast a clout 'til May is out*". 'Clout' is an ancient term for an outer layer of clothing, and the warning of this maxim is that when the white blossom of the May tree (the Hawthorn bush, *Crataegus monogyna*), not the month of May, unfurls then nature is prepared for the unfolding of the warmer weather and less cold nights. The wise person is un-likely to put away the winter warmers until May bushes flower white and pink!

Another sign from the trees that I have found to be almost unerringly true over several decades is that willow leaves turn over about twenty minutes before it is going to a rain. When I was first told about this in the late 1980s, I dismissed it as at best a myth and at worse a joke at my expense. But then it rained heavily almost exactly twenty minutes later – I had timed it on my watch! – and I began to take far greater notice about what the willow trees were doing when I was out in an exposed river valley. As we know, willow leaves, particularly the elongated leaves of the Crack Willow (*Salix fragilis*), flutter in a breeze. But they do also turn notably over as they flutter, exposing more of the felted covering of fine, silky white hairs on their undersides as rain is approaching. I have seen no scientific study of this – perhaps it is an adaptation for the water-repellent hairs to help it shed rainwater rapidly? – but I can certainly confirm from decades of empirical observation that willows do indeed forewarn us of rain about twenty minutes away!

Another country tale often told is that a greater profusion of red berries, particularly on Holly bushes (the English Holly, *Ilex aquifolium*, is one of 400-600 holly species worldwide), foretells of a cold winter approaching. Again, scientific studies seem to be lacking, though my experience is that this tale is a little less reliable than other tales surrounding trees.

One thing that trees do tell us is that the climate is most definitely changing. Oak buds burst and many tree seeds push up their first shoots now some weeks in advance of when they did several decades ago. Insects feeding upon this vegetation may or may not synchronise their timings, putting at risk the primary food of birds foraging to feed their springtime chicks and potentially disrupting important pollination and pest predation functions. Breaking down nature's time-hewn adaptations has serious risks for the workings of the natural world, and the benefits that it confers upon humanity.

Why does nature know best? Simply, it has evolved to respond to signals not evident to our finest analytical equipment, and is a 'moveable feast'. The timing of Easter, determined in 325CE by the Council of Nicaea as happening on the first Sunday after the first Full Moon occurring on or after the vernal equinox, is a crude human version of a 'moveable feast' but lacking nature's highly adapted sensitivity.

Mother Nature is so much wiser than us mere evolutionary upstarts, 3.85 billion years of fine-tuning meaning that she has many tricks to teach us!

MARCH OF THE
KILLER LOBSTERS

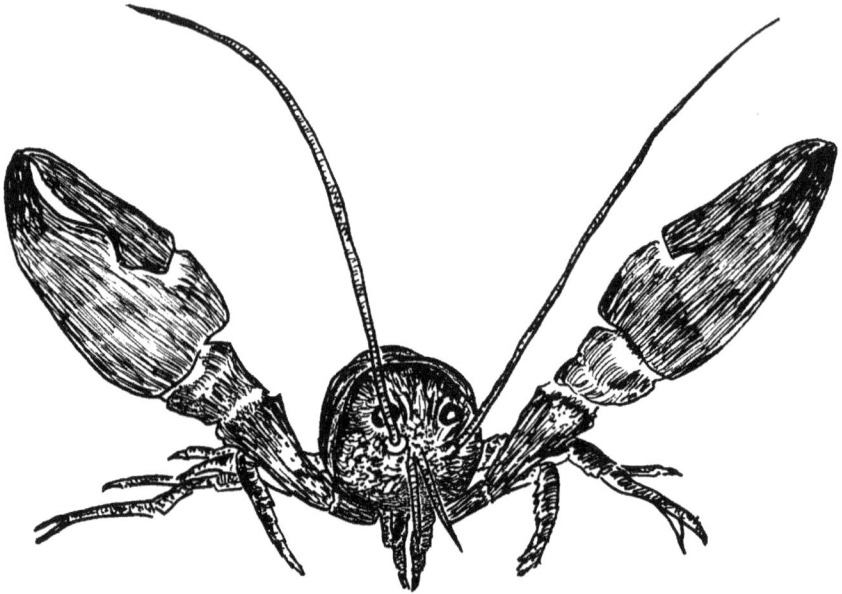

M Y HOME RIVER, the Bristol Avon, like so many across Britain,, used
to play host to a charismatic little crustacean. Over a quarter-century
ago, the White-clawed Crayfish (*Austropotamobius pallipes*) graced us with
its presence, scavenging the river's bed. That was, until the march of the killer
lobsters.

The American Signal Crayfish (*Pacifastacus leniusculus*) was introduced
to Europe in the 1960s, to be cropped for the food market. Introductions of
organisms beyond their native range and the ecosystems with which they
co-evolved can lead to their genes, like genies uncorked from bottles, becoming
unpredictable when released from the bottlenecks of natural checks and
balances, such as predation, parasites and diseases. Their life habits may also
not mesh with the dynamics of their new environments. From Himalayan
Balsam (*Impatiens glandulifera*) plants widespread along river banks to
fish species such as the Common Carp (*Cyprinus carpio*) and invertebrates
including the Signal Crayfish, bad things can happen when these species run
amok.

Not only is this American cousin bigger and more aggressive than the native crayfish, seeing it off in a straight fight for territory and food, it also carries a fungal disease – 'Crayfish Plague' (*Aphanomyces astaci*) – to which it is a resistant carrier but which is 100% fatal to our native White-clawed Crayfish. In late 2015, we lost the last remnant population of White-clawed Crayfish across the Bristol Avon catchment, a plague outbreak causing a complete kill on the By Brook tributary that had been its last stronghold. Straggling populations in other tributaries such as the Semington Brook, upper Tetbury Avon and around Sherston had been extirpated over previous decades.

The march of the Signal Crayfish continues across the country. Conservation measures beyond basic biosecurity to slow further spread now resort to establishing 'arc' populations of White-clawed Crayfish in suitable disused quarries and pits isolated from streams, against a time – who knows when as we yet lack the means – when the plague is eradicated.

From the pattern of 'invasions' across the Bristol Avon catchment, as within and between other drainage basins, it appears many new populations have been seeded by intentional translocations, most likely by unscrupulous players who return later to trap growing numbers for a tidy profit selling to the catering trade.

The spread of 'killer lobsters' matters for more than altruistic concern for a native species. Loss of White-clawed Crayfish now from much of the country should cause alarm, indicating a breakdown in the vitality and functioning of ecosystems from which we derive water and purification processes, amenity and heritage, and wider dimensions of environmental quality and resources. The Signal Crayfish is a voracious predator of fish eggs and soft-bodied invertebrates, also uprooting and eating water plants, and so further degrading the character and functioning of ecosystems we rely on for our health, economic resources and quality of life. They also burrow into river banks, reducing their stability and increasing erosion.

It is hard or impossible to put genies and genes back once out of their bottles. Globally, the spread of alien invasive species of plants, microbes, invertebrates and higher animals compounds local extinctions as part of a mass biotic homogenisation. It is vital we do all we can to halt the spread of 'killer lobsters' and other non-native species that potentially threaten rivers and other ecosystems underwriting our continuing wellbeing.

As a coda to this alarming tale, I also welcome the return of the Otter elsewhere in this book. One large male not uncommonly emerges to hunt near dusk – he is entirely fearless and can do so right under my feet – leaving the fish alone and instead rooting out and crunching loudly on Signal Crayfish. Thanks, Mr Otter, for exerting some control on a recently established Signal Crayfish population that is becoming problematic!

MAY

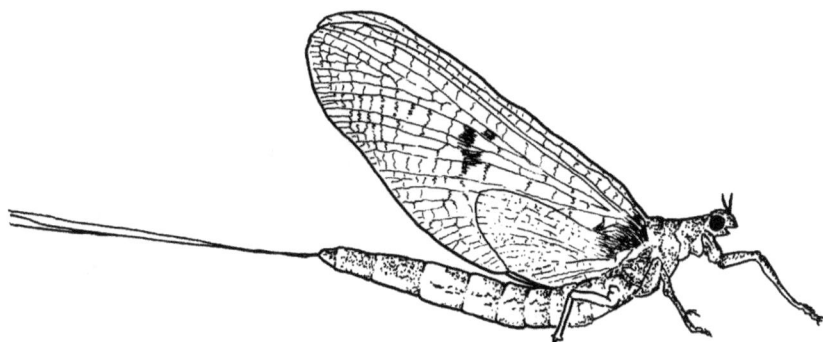

DANCE OF THE
'BOINGY-BOINGY
FLIES'

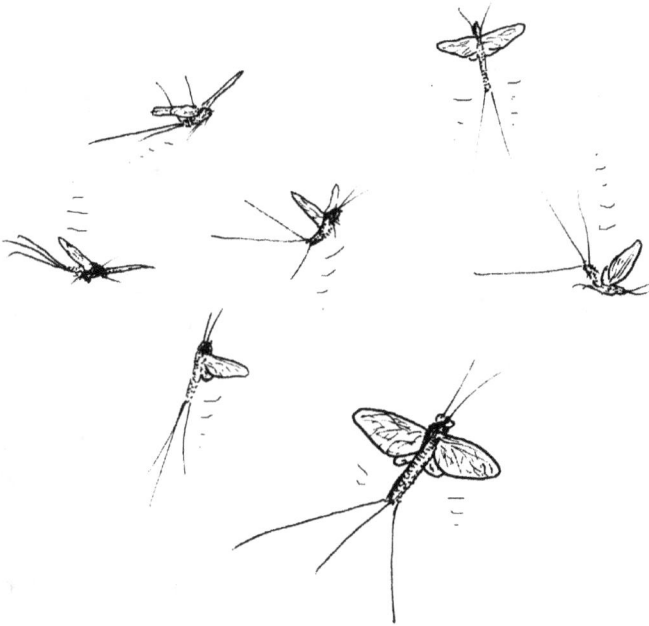

YOU KNOW THE ones I mean. Those dark-winged insects with long tail filaments that yo-yo around over grasslands by the river, increasingly as evening encroaches. Our friends gave them this name, a kind of visual onomatopoeia, and it has stuck.

The same is true for the 'daffy ducks' that work the river edge for small fish and large insects, often in pairs or small family groups. They are properly known as Dabchicks, or Little Grebes (*Tachybaptus ruficollis*). However, one of my late angling friends was, putting it generously, not a world-leading ornithologist and could hardly tell a Coot from a Wren. John though always knew his 'daffy ducks'. That name too stuck, part affectation but also apt descriptor of their erratic behaviour.

And so to the 'boingy-boingy flies', Britain's biggest mayfly species (*Ephemera danica*), also known as 'Green Drake' to fly anglers. Mayflies emerge *en masse* around May. That said, I once saw a small emergence one Boxing Day proving that, like fish, they don't read what we write about them.

Famously, mayflies live for a day. Actually, this is not true; they live for one or two years depending on climate and food availability. Mostly, this is as larvae out of sight in the river bed, feeding on detritus and going through a series of moults after hatching from eggs through to near-completion of their life cycles.

Then, one warm day when conditions suit, the larvae swim up to the surface, splitting their skins to allow the winged subimago, or 'dun', to burst free from the surface film in seconds. (There is no pupal phase, just free-flying sub-adult and fully adult forms.) These duns lift from the water to seek refuge generally on the undersides of leaves of riverside trees.

This is a time of mass carnage or, to their predators, of feast. Many larvae never complete the hazardous swim to the surface, engulfed by hungry fish. More insects are taken as they seek to burst free from the now imprisoning husk of their final larval skin. Many that fly clear are strafed by Swallows, House Martins and Swifts, Chiffchaffs and other warblers, House Sparrows, Grey Wagtails and many more. Spiders take their toll as duns shelter in tree canopies. But, by sheer numbers, some make it through to the following day.

Then, the final metamorphosis occurs as the fully mature adult form, the imago, bursts from the skin of the dun to take to the late spring air and dance over floodplain grasslands.

Why do they flaunt themselves so conspicuously with myriad predators keen on an easy meal, 'boingy-boinging' flagrantly in broad daylight and into dusk? The answer is that this is dance of sexual ecstasy, females releasing pheromones (hormones outside the body) to attract males. Watch the 'boinging' swarm and you will see some insects coupling briefly in the air as they fall.

Then their lives are all but done. The females 'boing' again over water, dipping their abdomens into the water to release batches of fertilised eggs that fall to the river bed to perpetuate the cycle.

Then, they die. Spent adults, known as 'spinners', fall to the water's surface with wings splayed, often accumulating in mats, and fish feast in a gluttonous orgy on their nutritious corpses. To anglers, this is known as

'Duffers Fortnight', when even the least competent fly fisher can cast an imitation fly on a dead drift and expect to fool fish in a feeding frenzy.

The order of insects comprising the mayflies has the Latin name *Ephemeroptera*, reflecting the ephemeral appearance of the magnificent adult form. But in reality the insect is relatively long-lived down there in the silty river bed, its large and nutritious larvae a staple diet of Barbel (*Barbus barbus*) and other bottom-feeding fish.

And the emerging mayfly, of course, is a promise of spring segueing into warmer, longer days with the promise of the unfurling of nature's lush and easy summer splendour.

THE WHITE MONTH

I SOMETIMES THINK of May as the white month.

There have already been white blossoms, some of them now past their peak such as the Blackthorn, painting the hedgerows and meadows by the river and across the wider countryside. However, May blows in on a froth of white flowers.

There is of course the May tree itself: the Hawthorn (*Crataegus monogyna*) and the opening of its white flowers that is the basis of the countryside saying "*Ne'er cast a clout 'til May is out*" (never shed your winter clothes until the May tree blossom, not the month of May, is out). But this is also the month when the frothy white umbels of Cow Parsley (*Anthriscus sylvestris*) are at their most profuse in the hedgerows, joined throughout the month by those of the Pignut (*Conopodium majus*) and Common Hogweed (*Heracleum sphondylium*), and later on the tall Hemlock (*Conium maculatum*).

In open ground, the Common Daisy (*Bellis perennis*) and the white 'clocks' of Dandelion (*Taraxacum agg.*) seed heads whiten the sward, very soon augmented by White Clover (*Trifolium repens*) and various chickweeds, joined in drier slopes by Ox-eye Daisies (*Leucanthemum vulgare*). In hedgerows and coarser turf, White Dead-nettles (*Lamium album*) show their off-white blossom where various stitchwort species share their delicate, star-shaped flowers.

In wet and shaded ground, the fresh flowers of Ramsons (*Allium ursinum*), also known as Wild Garlic, Wood Garlic and Bear's Garlic, show through stark white, replacing the delicate white-blooming Wood Anemones (*Anemone nemorosa*). Comfrey (*Symphytum officinale*) plants thrust upwards, opening their flowers both white and purple. In the cooler margins of hedges, the tips of Jack-by-the-hedge – known by so many regional names including Garlic Mustard, Garlic Root, Hedge Garlic, Sauce-alone, Jack-in-the-bush, Penny Hedge and Poor Man's Mustard – are dusted with small white crucifer flowers. Jack-by-the-hedge plants are visited by female Orange-tip butterflies, all white with black points lacking the vivid orange forewing tips of the male insect, laying their eggs on this favoured food plant upon which their caterpillars will gorge. The Maytime air too is visited by increasing numbers of off-white female Brimstone butterflies, lacking the sulphur-yellow of the males that have already been on the wing for a fortnight or perhaps more.

Surrounding scrub, hedgerows and copses are painted by the whites and soft pinks of Crab Apples and Wild Cherry joined, on the limey soils of our Cotswold edge villages, by the white flower heads of Wayfaring trees and, on more neutral or acidic soils, by the first Rowan blossoms. Later in the month, Elder and Guelder-rose panicles join the white vista, along with the blossoms of dog roses and early brambles clambering up woody supports towards the sunlight. Beyond them and by the river's edge, white 'candlestick' florets adorn majestic Horse Chestnut trees.

But, though the spectrum of whites might be prominent in this month, nature is far from monochrome. Indeed, this is the month of diversifying, intensifying and contrasting hues on plants, birds and other beasties beyond the range and imagination of even the finest human artist.

Greens from the cool yellow-green of Oak and Ash leaves freshly emerging from buds darken as the month progresses, contrasting with deep green Ivy, the red-tinged tips of fresh Hawthorn shoots and countless verdant tones between and beyond as spring unfolds to a crescendo. The scrub is excited by the vivid reds of campion, and the sward by the buttery yellows of buttercups and Cowslip. The deep blues of Bluebells and speedwells contrast with the similar hues of the spring brood of Holly Blue butterflies. Other brown butterflies paddle the riverside air, from Speckled Woods in the dappled shade and the first Meadow Browns over open grassland.

We live truly in a wonderland, even in this whitest of months of unfolding spring.

DANDELION CLOCKS

I T IS THAT time of year again when the meadows by the riverside
and across the wider countryside are adorned with the fluffy heads of
'Dandelion Clocks'. We probably all played the Dandelion clock game as
children, picking the downy, spherical seed heads of a Dandelion and blowing
away the seeds to find out what time it was: how many puffs does it take and
there you have the time!

The Dandelion derives its name from the serrated edge of the leaves,
growing as a low rosette from a strong tap root rendering them resistant
to grazing pressure. The derivation of the name is from the French 'dent-
de-lion', meaning 'lion's tooth', referring to those toothed leaves. There are
multiple species of Dandelions around the world, all in the genus *Taraxacum*.
However, there is widespread genetic mixing, so it is hard to define exactly
where one 'species' ends and another begins, hence the common assignment of
the Dandelions we know and love as *Taraxacum agg.* (short for 'aggregation'
in common with various plant species with similarly fluid genetics). However,
many *Taraxacum* species produce seeds asexually, without pollination,
resulting in offspring that are genetically identical to the parent plant. Various
cultivars have also been bred for the horticultural trade.

Dandelions belong within the daisy family (Asteraceae, formerly known as the Compositae) on the basis of their composite flowering heads. Each 'flower' is in fact a compact floret comprising many tightly packed individual flowers. There are some 32,913 accepted species in the family Asteraceae, ranging from low-growing annuals to trees, the latter particularly in the tropics, making it one of the largest and most widespread plant families.

The two most common Dandelion species across the temperate world are *Taraxacum officinale* and *Taraxacum erythrospermum*, but most of their global range today results from accidental and sometimes deliberate introductions from Europe. Dandelions were, for example, deliberately introduced into Australia and various other European colonial territories by 'Acclimatisation Societies' that encouraged the introduction of familiar species to new countries around the world to enrich their perceived 'impoverished' flora and fauna. This pre-Darwinian thinking was that all in creation was made at a set time, and only the most favoured countries (ours!) had the full set, so our solemn duty was to fill in the gaps in other countries where they were as yet missing! Fill in the gaps we did with vigour, the best of intentions, massive naivety and significant consequential disastrous outcomes!

Though the common Dandelion is generally overlooked, or regarded in gardens or farmland and as an undesirable weed, these plants in fact have some remarkable properties.

All parts of a Dandelion are edible, and Dandelions have been gathered for food since prehistory. Leaves can be used directly in salads, or else blanched or lightly cooked like spinach to remove bitterness. Dandelion leaves and buds are part of traditional cuisines in regions and countries as diverse as Kashmir, Slovenia, China and Korea. Dandelion flowers have traditionally been used to make Dandelion wine, whilst ground and roasted Dandelion roots form the basis of caffeine-free Dandelion coffee. Many may remember 'Dandelion and Burdock', the traditional British soft drink, and Dandelions are also an ingredient of root beer. The Latin generic name *Taraxacum* itself originates from medieval Persian writings recording that "...*the tarashaquq is like chicory*".

Dandelions also had many medicinal uses. The English folk name 'piss-a-bed' mirrors the contemporary French name 'pissenlit', referring to the strong diuretic effect of Dandelion roots. Dandelions contain a diversity of pharmacologically active compounds, and have been used in many herbal remedies across Europe, North America and China, including for treating infections, bile and liver problems in addition to their diuretic properties. However, Dandelion pollen can cause allergic reactions in sensitive individuals.

The latex secreted from Dandelion stems and leaves when cut or broken can also cause allergic reactions. However, latex production has been enhanced in a Dandelion cultivar developed in Germany for commercial production of natural rubber of equivalent quality to that derived from rubber trees.

Dandelions also, of course, play many roles in the functioning of ecosystems including as sources of seeds for birds, a pump of nutrients from deeper soil layers via their long tap roots, a food plant for various butterfly and moth larvae, and a source of nectar for other insects.

We may know them as lawn weeds or 'Dandelion Clocks' in a May meadow. We may call them by myriad local names including Blowball, Cankerwort, Doon-head-clock, Witch's Gowan, Milk Witch, Lion's-tooth, Yellow-gowan, Irish Daisy, Monks-head, Priest's-crown, Puff-ball, Faceclock, Pee-a-bed, Wet-a-bed, Swine's Snout, White Endive or Wild Endive. But we should not dismiss the commonplace Dandelion as, whilst their characteristic 'clocks' may be unreliable timepieces, these everyday plants serve our needs and support our wellbeing in so many other ways.

A HEALTHY
RIVERSIDE WALK

M Y RESEARCH IN the developing world, particularly on Himalayan rivers, is always testing and especially given certain medical limitations on my mobility. But, whatever the hardship, I know I always come back feeling fantastic. In fact, a healthy walk by any river can be relied on for such an outcome.

Back in 1984, American scientist Roger Ulrich published a study of how patients in hospital beds with views of vegetation, and particularly of water, experienced dramatically improved surgical recovery rates compared to those with urban views. The evidence base correlating exposure to nature with various parameters of physical and mental health – pulse rate, blood pressure, anxiety, social inclusion, concentration, etc. – has subsequently grown substantially and persuasively. Health professionals take the benefits of nature exposure increasingly into consideration, with various UK Primary Care Trusts – Devizes in Wiltshire amongst them – as well as health authorities in places from Scotland to New Zealand prescribing 'green exercise' as an effective treatment for a variety of physical and mental conditions.

We feel many of these effects ourselves when striding out by the river. Our lungs expand, our blood pumps faster, our lymph systems get flushed, and our eyes relax to take in wider and more distant vistas after prolonged, fixed-distance focus on close-up screens. Birdsong and the sibilance of zephyrs ruffling the trees, the kaleidoscope of natural colours, odours of moist earth, greenery and musty scent trails, wind in our hair and the sense of impending rain all reward and renew the senses. Then there are the beneficial effects of socialisation whether through walking with companions, the happenchance of meeting other people, or encounters with myriad non-human life forms.

Today, there is increasing recognition of 'nature deficit disorder', describing the human costs of alienation from the natural world due to the growing psychological and behavioural disconnection of people, younger people in particular, from the ecosystems upon which we depend and with which we co-evolved. Whilst not (at least yet) a defined medical condition, 'nature deficit disorder' is certainly acknowledged as contributing to a range of health issues from short-sightedness and poor posture due to excessive time staring at computer screens, hypertension, and conditions such as obesity and diabetes resulting from a sedentary life style. American evolutionary biologist E.O. Wilson takes this concept further under the concept of 'Biophilia', recognising our deeper connections with and dependence upon the ecosystems with which we co-evolved for sound physical and mental health, extrapolating this thinking to conjecture how the disconnections of contemporary lifestyles contribute to society's tacit acquiescence to unsustainable and antisocial behaviours.

Financial valuation of the benefits afforded by a healthy walk by the river is far from straightforward. However, tangible sums are associated with the uplifted value of commercial and residential property in proximity to 'green' and 'blue' (watery) spaces and the costs of treatment of conditions exacerbated by lack of 'green exercise'. Other values are far less quantifiable, yet are nonetheless palpable, invaluable and perhaps even priceless.

In whatever terms they are accounted, the multiple values of a healthy walk by the river are substantial, life affirming and above all free; yet another of the gifts from nature with which we are so blessed.

A RIOT OF GRASSES

L IKE MANY OF us, I was once oblivious to the theatre of grasses. Grasses were grasses, all seemingly much alike and merging into a green sward. Even in those days when I really had my eye in on most of the rest of the British flora – a familiarity now too much diluted by work on Asian and African ecosystems with time at home overly tied to a computer – grasses, like girls when I was an early teenager, resolutely evaded my attempts to gain more intimate acquaintance.

But this was suddenly to change when I decided that enough was enough, investing a day into a grass identification course run by my local county Wildlife Trust. It was as if a veil had been lifted from my eyes, suddenly to be helped to discern and thence to appreciate such diversity and dramatic differences formerly obscured by the density of my ignorance.

The closest parallel I can draw is the contemporary music fan who protests that "*All classical music sounds the same*", but with coaxing and coaching enters a formerly hidden universe of soaring symphonies, delicate chamber ensembles, virtuoso solo renditions and profound requiems.

There is a joy in watching the ever-changing carousel of grasses as spring and summer evolve on river banks and riparian meadows. The names of the grasses alone are a poem to the turning of the seasons.

Spikey heads of Sweet Vernal Grass (*Anthoxanthum odoratum*) flower early and low, this grass offering fresh hay its sweet aroma. The one-sided heads of Crested Dog's-tail (*Cynosurus cristatus*) also rise low to the turf on drier mounds.

By May's end, taller bushy foxtails (*Alopecurus* species) – like many grasses so-named for their resemblance – join the ever-taller sward adding structure to the kaleidoscope of flowering buttercups and red-tipped sorrels. Joining the thickening throng of greenery come the pointed flower heads of brome (*Bromus* species), sharp as beech buds. So too, the characteristic lobes of Cock's-foot (*Dactylis glomerata*), also named for their visual similarity.

Taller still, fescues (*Festuca* species) reach skywards for light, holding their broom of flowers and seeds aloft. By roadsides and drier slopes, robust clumps of False Oat-grass (*Arrhenatherum elatius*) rise tall and tough.

In paths and shaded edges, the robust Perennial Ryegrass (*Lolium perenne*) shows its glossy coat, whilst the diaphanous feathers of *Poa* heads fan out in the summer air.

As June arrives, glaucous clusters of Yorkshire Fog (*Holcus lanatus*) unveil their mist-like heads to breathe pollen into the warming summer air. Keen eyes pick out the delicate lanterns of Quaking Grass (*Briza* species), quivering on zephyrs.

These and more grasses rise in succession to dominate the sward for their often brief moment in the sun, an orchestra in the meadow commencing with a quiet overture, swelling and enriching with growing heat and light to the crescendo of full summer.

And this is before we savour the lushness of Sweet Reed-grass (*Glyceria maxima*) and Reed Canary Grass (*Phalaris arundinacea*) marching from dry land into the river's edge, Flote Grass (*Glyceria fluitans*) blades emerging from river sediments to the languid surface to lie flat in margins of the summer river, and the tall bur-reeds (*Sparganium* species) with their stellar flower heads in the margins and middle of the river.

Would that there were column inches enough to celebrate the diversity of sedges too!

When one sees beyond their superficial green uniformity, the riot of grasses reveals itself as outstandingly varied in form, function and utility for wildlife and people alike. Taking a moment to see beyond apparent sameness can only be enrichening for viewer and that which is viewed alike, nature once again serving us with a metaphor for life.

JUNE

WALKING ON WATER

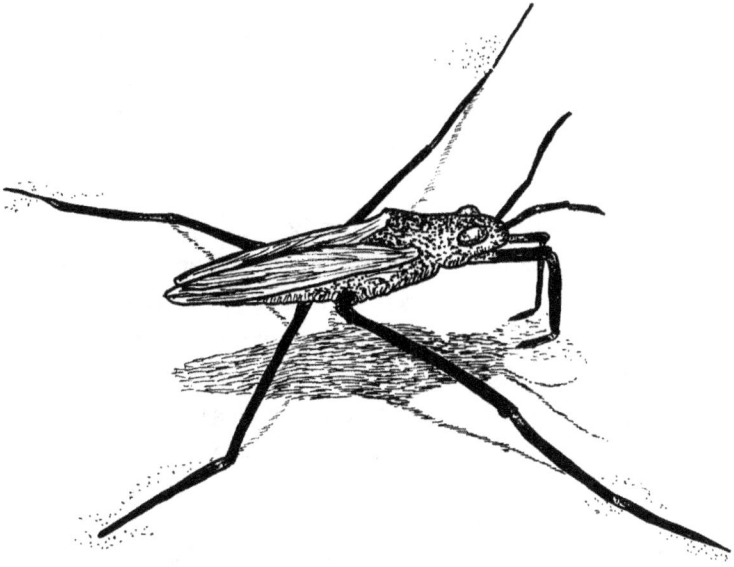

THE ABILITY TO walk on water is perceived as miraculous. I nearly did it once when a snake and I nearly swam into each other in the middle of a Sussex lake in the mid-1970s though, even in my blind panic, I didn't quite achieve escape velocity. However, a wide variety of creatures live their lives walking on water. One such common insect on our river and local pools is the Pond Skater.

How do Water Measurers, Whirligig Beetles, various flies and all manner of other beasties, many heavier than water, manage the seemingly impossible of not merely alighting on water without sinking, but also propelling themselves to hunt, mate and evade predation?

This is largely due to the extraordinary properties of water. Water molecules, as we know, comprise two atoms of hydrogen and one of oxygen. This makes them polar, with positively charged hydrogen atoms attracted to negatively charged oxygen atoms in neighbouring water molecules forming a kind of semi-crystalline structure. Hence, it takes a lot of energy to break these bonds when turning water into steam, and falling water breaks up into internally attracted drops. At the surface of a water body, molecules are attracted to others below but not to the air above. This creates the phenomenon of surface tension, effectively forming a 'skin' on the water's surface. It is on this skin that these beasties walk, generally aided by hydrophobic (water-repelling) body surfaces.

OK, that's the physics lesson over. Now to the Pond Skaters, often seen resting or skating on the surface film of pools and slacker river margins on four of their outstretched legs. They also sense the surface film for fine ripples generated by the struggles of trapped insects. Once detected, Pond Skaters propel themselves at speed to the commotion for a meal. (You can trick them into hunting a grass stem by gently wiggling it in the surface film.) Pond Skaters belong to a group of insects known as 'bugs' (Hemiptera), lacking biting mouth parts but possessing instead a 'beak' that they stab into their prey to inject digestive enzymes, sucking out the pre-digested, liquefied contents. Pond Skaters also sense each other's movements through the surface film, exhibiting some social behaviours. This explains why you often see groups of these amazing water-walking animals. However, cannibalism is not uncommon when populations become dense and food scarce, smaller Pond Skater nymphs often falling prey to large adult insects.

Pond Skater populations increase throughout the spring and summer, but they are generally not visible in the winter as the adults hibernate usually near water and often in leaf litter or other similar refuges from meteorological extremes. Pond Skaters are also winged, sometimes flying between waters, particularly when populations become dense risking cannibalism, and also to move to and from hibernation sites.

Hibernating insects generally emerge from April onwards, though often earlier, vanishing again as the weather turns cold in October or November. Throughout their adult lives, pond Skaters lay eggs that hatch into a nymph form, superficially similar to adult insects but much smaller at around 1mm long. Nymphs progress through five instars (life stages between moulting their exoskeletons), getting progressively bigger until fully adult. The widespread native species, the Common Pond Skater (*Gerris lacustris*), is one of nine British species, generally reaching a length of around 1cm.

Next time you see one or a group of them, stop a while and marvel at these small creatures – also known as Water Striders, Water Bugs, Water Skippers or Jesus Bugs – as they artlessly perform yet another of nature's everyday miracles.

HALYCON DAYS

WITH PERHAPS MISPLACED optimism, I anticipate the calm, peaceful halcyon days of 'flaming June'. We know what we mean by 'halcyon days', don't we?

In Greek myth, Alcyone was the daughter of Aeolos, *God of the Winds*, and herself had power over the winds. Alcyone, or Halcyone, was a faithful lover marrying Ceyx, son of Heosphoros, the *Day Star* (from whom we derive the word 'Phosphorus'). But the Greek gods were vain, jealous and vengeful. Wanting Alcyone for himself, Zeus killed Ceyx by sinking his ship with a thunderbolt. Grief-stricken Alcyone threw herself into the sea to rejoin Ceyx in death. However, pitying them both, the other gods immediately turned both Alcyone and Ceyx into Kingfishers.

The halcyon is the Kingfisher, in all probability our familiar Eurasian or Common Kingfisher (*Alcedo atthis*). This elegant bird occurs from as far north as the Moray Firth in Scotland right down across the Mediterranean to the northern coast of Africa, across the Balkans and throughout Asia as far as Japan, and is a common sight also fishing rivers on which I work throughout India.

The Greek legend continues – entirely unfounded in any biological reality I might add – that Kingfishers build a nest of fish bones upon the surface of the sea. At this time, either Alcyone or her father (versions of the legend vary) exerts their power over the waves to produce calm seas in these 'halcyon days'. This is not, as in our common parlance, the balmy days of summer but actually seven days prior to and then following the winter solstice. These are the 'halcyon days' of peace and calm at sea that, legend still has it, remain commonplace around the winter solstice on the Mediterranean.

This is not all good news for the Kingfisher. A now largely abandoned practice amongst sailors was to hang a dead Kingfisher on board their ship to know the direction of the wind.

Other legends relate that the Kingfisher was once a dull, grey bird. Some say its dazzling colours stem from biblical times when, along with the Dove and the Raven, the Kingfisher was the first bird to leave Noah's Ark searching for dry land. In variants of the tale, the Kingfisher caught the red rays of the sun on its breast and the azure of the sky on its back to attain its gaudy appearance. Under another version, the pioneering Kingfisher gained the vivid blue on its back on being struck by lightning, acquiring the fiery colour on its chest from flying too close to the sun. Another myth, with the kind of parallels one often finds in ancient tales from around the world, has it that the dull Kingfisher stole a burning brand of fire from the gods after a great flood, the fire catching the small bird aflame producing the burning colour of its chest plumage. None of these accounts quite tallies with Darwin's theory of evolution!

Sadly, the Kingfisher historically suffered for these myths and legends too. Ancient Greeks, for example, would hang a dead Kingfisher in the house in the belief that it would protect them from lightning. More recently, in various parts of Europe, the Kingfisher was seen as a lucky bird. Lucky, that is, for people and not for the bird itself! The hanging of a Kingfisher's feather around the neck was considered to confer protection from lightning and also negative energies, to act as a good luck charm, and to bring good health. Furthermore, to hear the call of a Kingfisher coming from the right was seen by some as a positive omen of imminent success in business, whilst the opposite is true from the left.

By June, Kingfishers are mid-way through the four to six months
(depending on climate) during which they pair and breed, brooding their
eggs in tunnels dug deep into vertical banks. Kingfishers are only partially
migratory, dividing paired summer territories into individual territories
to maximise available food and remaining resident throughout winter.
Consequently, the Kingfisher is known as the 'Ice Bird' in many countries:
Eisvogel in German, *Ijsvogel* in Dutch, and *Isfugl* in Danish and Norwegian.
Cold winters often take a dreadful toll on Kingfisher populations, as can
summer floods inundating their nests. But Kingfishers are adapted to recover
from these events through a high fecundity strategy. Pairs of Kingfisher
rear broods each of seven young, up to three times throughout a warm year,
enabling rapid population recovery.

British poet William Henry Davies wrote of the Kingfisher: "*It was the
Rainbow gave thee birth, And left thee all her lovely hues*". This is something
to dwell on by the river in these halcyon days, be they the balmy, summer
days we eagerly anticipate or, more accurately, around the winter solstice!

CHUBBY RIVER

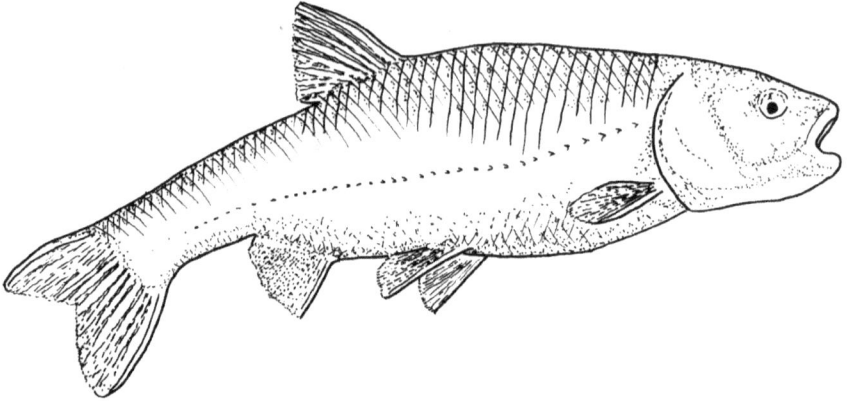

ONE OF THE more conspicuous fishes in many lowland rivers is the Chub (*Squalius cephalus*), frequently observed cruising the warm surface film during (allegedly) 'flaming June' days and throughout the summer.

A member of the carp and minnow family (Cyprinidae), Chub are 'chubby' in build. This probably accounts for their currently common name, though historic names include 'Chevin', 'Chevander' and 'Loggerhead'. Chub are robust fish of flowing waters, though can prosper but not breed in still waters. Body profile is streamlined, rounded in cross-section and evenly covered with large, brassy and conspicuous scales. The dorsal (back) and tail (caudal) fins are dark, appearing charcoal-grey when Chub are spotted near the surface, whilst fins on the underside (paired ventral and single anal fins) are reddish.

One of the Chub's striking features is the cavernous, white-lipped mouth. Of all Britain's freshwater fishes, Chub are perhaps the most omnivorous, happy to engulf almost any plant or animal matter. Foods include detritus (amorphous organic matter rich in microorganisms), soft plants, blackberries, elderberries and the seeds and overwintering buds of waterside plants, worms, adult and larval insects, snails and mussels, small fishes, amphibians and even small swimming mammals. Chub are far from choosy, engulfing any available food from the bed, mid-water or surface, and notably more predatory as the water warms.

A Chub's mouth lacks barbels (sensory whiskers) and teeth. Instead, like all cyprinids, Chub have powerful pharyngeal teeth, located deep in their throat as modifications of gill rakers (internal protrusions from the gills). They use these to crush hard food items. NEVER put your finger down a Chub's throat, not merely as the fish won't like it, but because those powerful teeth may crush your fingertip like a seed, shell or small animal!

Chub are also often highly visible when shoaling to spawn on shallows over well-flushed river gravels in late May or June (precise timing varies with weather and may not even occur in cold years). Spawning typically occurs early in the day. Female Chub disturb open gravels into which their sticky eggs fall, males fertilising them with milt as they settle. Siltation of gravels from poor agricultural practices and urban run-off has severe consequences for spawning success of Chub and other gravel-spawning species. Disturbed patches of gravel at the tails of weirs and other well-flushed reaches are tell-tale signs of recent spawning, shoals of minnows often gathering conspicuously to feast on the nutritious eggs which receive no parental care.

Chub fry hatch still attached to yolk sacs, which they consume before becoming free-swimming after a few days. The fry require warm, shallow marginal water rich in small food items to grow quickly enough to withstand winter spates. Cool summers with poor growing conditions often result in the loss of most juveniles by year end, creating pronounced 'year classes' in Chub populations reflecting optimal nursery conditions over previous summers. Juveniles feed on algae and small invertebrates, older fish becoming increasingly omnivorous as they grow.

Smaller Chub can be confused with Dace (*Leuciscus leuciscus*). However, aside from the more delicate mouth of the Dace, fin shapes also differ: the outer edge of the Chub's dorsal and anal fins are convex (bulge outwards) whilst those of the Dace are concave (bending inwards).

For the aspirant 'fish twitcher', Chub are one of our more readily-spotted freshwater fishes. Chub-spotting requires no special access or equipment, though polarised sunglasses help cut through glare from the river's surface. A stealthy approach is vital, particularly avoiding heavy footfalls transmitting vibrations from bank to water, and avoiding betraying your presence by showing your silhouette against the skyline.

RIVERS OF PEACE

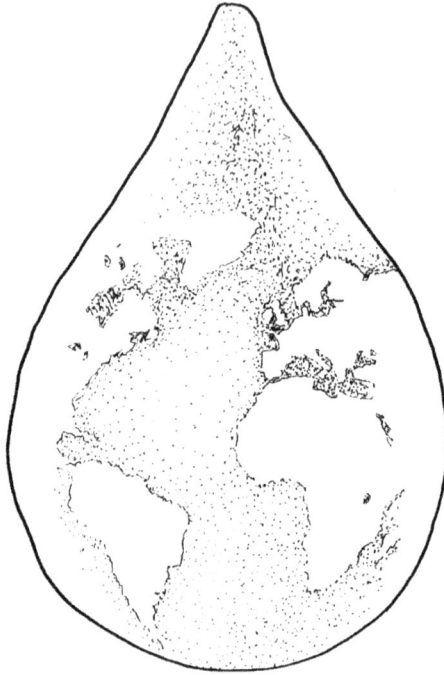

I T IS PEACEFUL to watch the river's water flowing by, and reassuring to
know that groundwater flows unseen beneath our feet through permeable
soils and rock strata. But this situation does not occur everywhere.

In some of the arid regions where I work in India and Africa, rivers may
run only during and immediately after sporadic, seasonally bounded monsoon
rainfall, and careful stewardship may be essential to maintain accessible, pure
groundwater throughout the remainder of the year. It is not uncommon
for excessive water extraction and/or pollution to seriously constrain the
availability of adequate clean water, the poorest in society often suffering the
greatest water poverty. Elsewhere, dams may be built to appropriate the
energy and water within river flows, diverting them to economically and
politically powerful urban and industrial centres, but with the unfortunate
collateral consequence of fragmenting catchments, depleting downstream
river reaches and disadvantaging their many marginalised dependants. Not
infrequently, these 'water grabs', including both actual or perceived inequitable

exploitation of water flows, span international borders and have been a source of international friction or conflict.

Ismail Serageldin, then World Bank Vice President, stated in 1995 that "...if the wars of this century were fought over oil, the wars of the next century will be fought over water, unless we change our approach to managing this precious and vital resource". The sentiment rings true, and is often repeated. However, the reality is that water-related conflicts are nothing new, having recurred throughout history. Conflicts are, at core, always about a limited resource of one kind or another, even when dressed as matters of ideology, faith, ethnicity or other. Water is and will increasingly become limiting in an increasingly populous, climate-changing world. The Six-Day War of 1967 between Israel and the Arab League was all about impoundment and annexation of the transboundary Jordan River and adjacent catchments. Drainage of the homeland swamps of the Marsh Arabs was a weapon of war wielded by Saddam Hussein, and Iraq's dams remain fiercely defended today. Flooding of the Ruhr Valley was a key objective of the Dambusters raids of the Second World War. Contested rights to the resource of transboundary rivers remain sources of potential conflict or threat today between India and Pakistan, Turkey and Syria, as well as across many neighbouring African nations.

However, the good and generally underreported news is that the conclusions of various analyses around the world find that international agreements relating to management and sharing of transboundary rivers, wetlands and lakes have far more frequently constituted a basis for maintaining or achieving peace between neighbouring states than they ever have as a spark for war.

The reality of our global future is that natural resources are in steep decline whilst the human population rises in a changing climate that influences the intensity and timing of rainfall.

The UK's Ministry of Defence is far from naïve about the importance of sustainable water and other natural resource stewardship in averting conflict and securing peace in this contested future, making the case repeatedly in its periodic *Global Strategic Trends* reports that assess looming potential security threats looking thirty years into the future. The United Nations too has, since the 1990s, argued that protecting and sharing natural resources, particularly water, is critical for peace and security, the UN Security Council holding its first ever official debate on water, peace and security in November 2016.

Perhaps we do not fully realise how fortunate we are to be able to spend time by dependably flowing waters. The peace we feel when doing so is a microcosm of the vital role that sufficient flows of fresh water play in securing peace on a geopolitical scale.

SNOW IN SUMMER

I N THE SUNNIER days of early June, warm sun flattering to deceive before the chill of night, there can be days of snow within touching distance of the summer solstice.

In some freak years, this is literally so. But, in any year, this is the time of gossamer drifts of white fluff wafting on the gentlest of breezes in the warmer and drier part of late afternoon. A dusting of downy whiteness can form a blizzard peppering the calm river's surface, and accumulating in drifts in downwind slacks where ducklings may dabble and fill their crops from the surface accumulation of down and the many other fragments of plant and small animal matter that it traps.

The tight catkins of springtime Sallow (*Salix caprea*), Osier (*Salix viminalis*) and Crack Willow (*Salix fragilis*) bushes extend from tight bundles into tresses, their cargo of downy seeds giving these trees a whitish sheen. In dry and warm conditions, they liberate their tiny seeds, each embedded within a nest of the finest down, to be borne aloft and afar by the whims of late spring zephyrs. Perhaps some may land in fertile, moist soil to put down the roots of another riparian thicket that will play host to generations of nesting birds, protecting them still throughout the depths of winter as their weave of barren twigs offers refuge from predatory Sparrowhawks. Leaves of the Sallow, also known as the Goat Willow, provide food for the caterpillars of moth species than any other plant, the willow's leaves feeding countless other insects too including some that may drop into the water below to be engulfed by Chub, Brown Trout and other fishes.

It is well know that the bark of willows (the genus of willows is named *Salix* in Latin) is a source of salicylic acid (or salicin), the precursor of the familiar non-steroidal anti-inflammatory drug aspirin (acetylsalicylic acid) widely used as an analgesic medication to treat pain, fever or inflammation. But in herbalism, the bark and other parts of willows have been exploited by countless generations stemming back into prehistory to treat a host of maladies including those pain-relieving properties for which aspirin is effective as well as deployed as a decongestant and a blood thinner, and for acne, aging skin and relieving menstrual cramps. Some constituents of willow bark are now being explored for their apparent efficacy in some forms of cancer.

Sallow bushes and other willows also serve us well by stabilising river banks, and so averting erosion and soil loss. Their often bright reddish-orange masses of underwater roots serve as havens for small fishes, also providing a valuable spawning medium for fish species such as Roach and Perch. Thick stands of Sallow and Osier also trap organic matter and fine sediment, progressively building soil and creating moist microclimates supporting a proliferation of Water Mint, Gypsywort, Yellow Iris, Starwort and Sweet Reed-grass, which in turn play host to a menagerie of damselfly and other insect larvae, water beetles, water boatmen and other bugs, as well as juvenile fishes, the things they eat, and the creatures that eat them.

Snow in summer is a gift from nature to be treasured, not merely for its beauty but as a symbol of new life and the eternal regeneration of all of the intimately interconnected facets of river life that it sustains.

JULY

FRAGMENTS OF WILDERNESS

WE LIVE IN a crowded world; more people with less space between, impinged upon 24/7 by pervasive media. Quiet, reflective time is a dwindling harbour as technology, noise and light pollution increasingly clamour for our attention. Today, wilderness is at a premium. There is perhaps nowhere better to find fragments of wilderness in our busy world than in river valleys, particularly during the hours of darkness.

River valleys can be great places to watch the stars, if perhaps not fully comparable with places I know and work in the Himalayas, deserts or out to sea. But, notwithstanding how profoundly different our rivers are now as compared to their truly natural state, our local river valleys are nonetheless some of the wildest places to be found in these crowded and over-illuminated islands.

One leaves behind the light pollution that disorients plants and animals, disrupting their diurnal habits and life cycles. Perturbation of natural rhythms, including adequate exposure to darkness, can be bad for us too; the World Health Organization has classified night shift working as a potential carcinogen due to disruption of hormone systems linked to diurnal cycles.

Sitting out in the dark hours during balmier months, perhaps stargazing or with fishing lines cast out as rational excuses for the less rational experience of simply being there, one feels aloneness though never being truly alone within the expanse of nature and the universe. It is a calming, humbling experience, resetting norms stressed by daily demands. Nature's quiet sounds are a placid backwash: the gentle gurgle of river currents, the sibilance of a breeze stirring aspen leaves, rustles from small unseen creatures, the staccato bark of a distant fox and the peep of a disturbed Moorhen. Eyes attune to the darkness, catching the sway of tall grasses, Hemlock and Teasels caressed by waterside zephyrs, and the silhouette of a night-flying owl or Grey Heron.

There is also the overhead vista of bright pinpricks against inky, velvet blackness. Stars and planets are profuse, more and more of them evident as one looks into what ostensibly seems to be dark gaps. Sometimes, one can watch the slow track of a satellite or an aeroplane high enough to be soundless. Looking into the darkness, not thinking but simply being, is a kind of communion with the timelessness of the universe, the calmer natural flows on terra firma, and the quieter part of oneself that is too often swamped by modern, urbanised lifestyles, be they in the city or indoors in the country, that disconnect us from our natural heritage.

We evolved in harmony with the places that serve our needs for food and water, beauty and inspiration, tranquillity and clean air. Contemporary lifestyles do not have their rhythm; the ways we make use of nature lack its delicate balances. The light, noise and odours of modern life – urgent, attention-demanding, oriented to comfort and immediate gratification rather than co-existence and connection – encroach on our innate stillness and connection with natural places. Current alarming declines of species, ecosystems and their capacities to support our future needs are a consequence of contemporary neglect of their value.

Worryingly, many now perceive darkness and solitude with fear, reframing nature as threat rather than healing essence within which to immerse oneself and as the core resource upon which we all depend?

Spending time reconnecting thus with one's natural heritage is valuable, opening and healing senses battered by the urgency of modern life. Staring into the dark spaces between the stars reconnects us to the infinite, enriching us through experiencing the humility of our infinitesimal smallness.

THE SERPENT IN OUR LANDSCAPE

T HE UPPER COURSE of the Bristol Avon coils through the village in
which I live and around a string of adjacent villages, serpent-like in both
its form and innate mobility.

Naturally, British rivers flowed as dynamic networks of channels
through valley bottom forests. Falling trees would block some channels,
river energy scouring new routes and open spaces providing varied habitat for

diverse wildlife. These energetic systems constantly forged new pathways to reticulate and reshape the landscape, running in braids through broad valleys.

Contemporary rivers differ markedly, generally constrained to single channels by residential, industrial and agricultural 'reclamation' of floodplains. However, the fundamental forces shaping rivers remain. We are reminded of this by flooding of inappropriately sited development (as described elsewhere, 'floodplains' are so named for clear and linguistically evident reasons!) and when rivers break out of the shackles we impose upon them to carve into riparian land.

The physical forces of river flows erode sediment in some places and deposit it in others, creating forever changing riverscapes to which a diversity of wildlife becomes adapted. Vertical cliffs are formed where flows erode and undercut banks, often on the outside of bends, presenting Kingfishers with ideal, safe places to tunnel out their nests. Silt bars form where slowing flows drop suspended sediment, creating nutrient-rich shallows that warm quickly in the sun promoting the rapid growth of fish fry and the small invertebrates upon which they depend.

If we had a multi-decadal time lapse camera, we would observe the serpentine river writhing in ever-changing form across the floodplain as intermittent spates or sustained flow energy reshape it, as they have for millennia. When the river is in spate, you can positively hear the surging waters gurgle and boil as all that energy fights the resistance of river banks and bed.

Rivers like the Wye or Severn channel huge energy from large upland headwater areas and steep gradients, often cutting through bends or forming new ones during major flood events. For smaller lowland rivers, these geomorphological (earth-forming) processes are less dramatic but forever present. My home river, like all others, fights the constraints of modern landscape management that tend, in practice, to focus its energy and erosive force.

In farmed land, it is generally accepted that some banks will be eroded whilst elsewhere there are gains through deposition. However, what happens when the serpent is pinned down by politics or possession?

Sometimes, rivers form administrative boundaries. It is common to see parish boundaries tracing old river courses rather than the current river's track though, in many cases, administrative boundaries follow its changing shape.

But what about riparian properties, defined by deed yet at risk of continued erosion? Nature's flows do not, of course, respond to mere human definitions and curtilages; ask the sadly misunderstood King Canute about that! The river bears us no malice, indeed delivers us many benefits, but its impersonal forces will not be denied.

We restrain the writhing serpent at various points along its course through our communities with different forms of bank reinforcement – gabions, rip-rap, concrete, bridge armouring, spiling, deflectors, sheet piling, and so forth – engineered to resist its erosive force and inclination to carve a new path that may not fit with static infrastructure or property boundaries imposed on an inherently dynamic landscape.

We also compound its tendency to erode land we want to protect by removing vegetation – shrubs, trees, reedy edges and other land cover – the root structure of which does much to stabilise soils and so resist erosion. We plant or permit the proliferation of non-native plants – Himalayan Balsam in particular in many reaches of British rivers – that displace native vegetation then die back in the fall to expose bare, more readily eroded riverside soil.

Sometimes, it is necessary to engineer structures to inhibit the river's natural mobility, averting property damage or loss. This can now be done with natural materials of greater sensitivity than the solutions dreamed of by our concrete-loving forebears. Better still, we should recognise that rivers are dynamic beasts that will not be readily tamed, and so learn to plan and invest in working synergistically with them rather than fighting them under an anachronistic supremacist Victorian ideal of 'taming nature'.

Nature in bigger than us, our benefactor and our neighbour. But, treat it like our servant and we might just find we have grabbed a serpent by the tail.

CHEMICAL WARFARE
BY THE RIVERSIDE

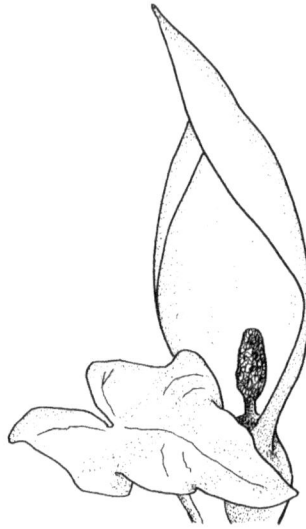

A SERENE RIVERSIDE walk amongst the lushness of late spring foliage and flowers is a wonderful thing, much to be recommended to bring you peace. However, you are in reality walking through a theatre of intense chemical warfare.

The herbal values as well as drug and poisonous qualities of many of our everyday riverside plants are considered elsewhere in *Riverwatch*. These include Britain's deadliest plant, Hemlock Water-dropwort (*Oenanthe crocata*) every part of which is potentially deadly, though this plant is extremely common along the banks of British rivers and other moist habitats. Also the Yew tree (*Taxus baccata*), also a far from uncommon plant, of which most parts are highly toxic including the leaves that remain so even when dried. However, the Yew is also the source of the molecule taxol – better known by its pharmacological name of Tamoxifen – which has powerful and now widely used anti-cancer properties that enhance the lives of many people around the world, significantly including survivors of breast cancer.

The Arum Lily (*Arum maculatum*) – widespread across Europe and with a host of common names including Cuckoo Pint, Snakeshead, Adder's Root, Arum, Wild Arum, Lords-and-Ladies, Devils and Angels, Cows and

Bulls, Adam and Eve, Bobbins, Naked Girls, Naked Boys, Starch-root, Wake
Robin, Friar's Cowl, Sonsie-give-us-your-hand, Jack-in-the-pulpit, and Cheese
and Toast – has a host of symbolic associations, many of which are reflected
in common names. Aside from its poisonous qualities (the Cuckoo Pint is said
to be one of the most common causes of accidental plant poisoning), the scent
emitted by the flower attracts the flies that help transfer pollen between plants.
Many other plants, as we know from the heady spring and summer scents of
Honeysuckle (*Lonicera* species), Wisteria, roses and many more familiar plants,
put out a more pleasing aroma to attract pollinators as diverse as butterflies and
moths, sawflies, bees, bats and other small mammals, wasps and many more
creatures whose antics help spread pollen.

   Why should we be surprised that organisms that can not run away from
others that might eat or parasitise them, or move bodily towards potential
mates, have evolved sophisticated alternative chemical means to address their
survival needs? Many plants have evolved adaptations to make themselves
distasteful or, as in the case of the coffee plant, to develop a substance that
sends would-be grazing insects into a shudder so that they fall off the bush (we
happen to like the stimulus of caffeine!) In fact, many of nature's static and
slow-moving members – plants and fungi, but also sessile and slow-moving
animals – have evolved ingenious chemical means to kill, dissuade, attract,
stimulate, repel or otherwise interact with the myriad life forms with which
they have co-evolved.

   The females of many moths, and in particular those species with a
totally flightless female such as the Winter Moth (*Operophtera brumata*),
are effectively chemical sirens, releasing pheromones (hormones outside of the
body) to call in male moths. Meanwhile, numerous moth caterpillars carry
poisons, and many other slow-moving invertebrates accumulate toxins from
the plants that they eat.

   In reality, plants are a lot more sentient and interactive than we give
them credit. They rely on a far wider range of chemical and other stimuli
than those discernible through the limitations of human senses, interacting in
multiple ways with other plants of the same and other species as well as with a
diversity of other life forms.

   As we pace the river banks, we wade through a chemical soup replete
with messages, about which we are almost wholly oblivious. Many life forms
of great importance and wonder exist well beyond the acuity of our naked
eyes, but the same too is true for all of our other senses.

FIFTY SHADES OF BROWN

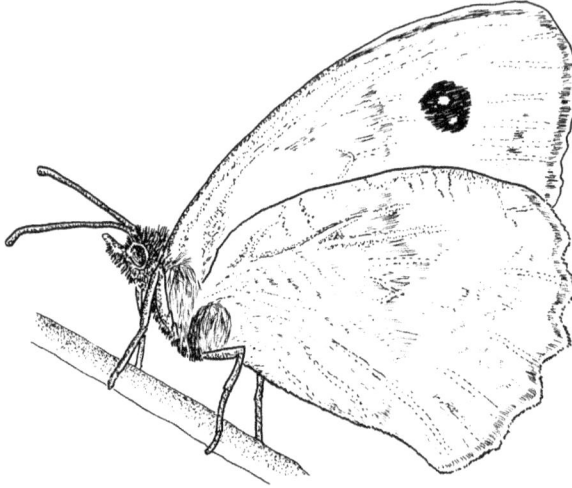

WITH SO MANY gaudy blossoms, birds and butterflies gracing our riverscape, it is perhaps odd to celebrate the palette of brown tones in this summer season. But open your eyes and a wonderful spectrum of textures and hues of brown come to the fore as July unfolds.

As grasses flower and dry, their haze of pollen and desiccated heads span all the tones from yellow to buff and deep bronze. Between them are the chocolate seed heads of Ribwort and, in taller stands, the now tan, desiccated panicles of Hemlock and Cow Parsley seeds held proudly aloft. Sorrel and dock hold high fox-red heads that deepen to crisp brown as the seeds dry and detach. And in the hedgerows, early-growing networks of Cleavers dry to buff straw now that their hooked and sticky seeds have set and, for many, been carried off on the fur of animals.

For me, the brown butterflies that emerge in this month to sport over and around the sward always bring joy. The most profuse of all these brown butterflies over the riverside meadows is the common but never commonplace Meadow Brown (*Maniola jurtina*), its jagged, erratic flight enabling confident identification from thirty years away, and even further when my eyes were younger.

And was there ever a more aptly named butterfly than the Gatekeeper (*Pyronia tithonus*), also known as appropriately as the Hedge Brown? This small, brown butterfly frequents hedgerows, particularly openings such as gates and styles, as a kind of small brown guard of honour.

On drier open grassland a little up the slope, Ringlet butterflies (*Aphantopus hyperantus*) appear with their bold 'string of pearls' dark eye spots around the margin on the deep brown wings. Closer to the sward, Small Skippers (*Thymelicus sylvestris*) hold their amber wings in characteristic x-wing orientation as they bathe in the summer sunshine, taking to the air at pace as you approach.

Flamboyantly-hued though the upper wings of many of the vanessids are – a group of brush-footed butterflies including the Small Tortoiseshell (*Aglais urticae*), Peacock (*Aglais io*), Red Admiral (*Vanessa atalanta*) and Comma (*Polygonia c-album*) butterflies all freshly minted as they take to the warm summer air – their underwings are muted dark browns and blacks offering excellent camouflage against bark and dry leaves as they lie at rest with wings folded erect above their backs.

River margins turn brown too with a film of diatoms and other algae, growing profusely on all surfaces as the sunlight illuminates and heats the sluggish water as flows decline. Around them, the textures and tones of willow, alder and ash bark and early-turning leaves add to the brownscape.

As dusk approaches, buff-toned sedge flies crawl up emergent stems to take to the cooling air, often in profusion. These moth-like insects spend as much as two years as aquatic larvae, some of them mobile, with or without protective cases around their soft bodies, and others cemented in cases to underwater rocks, wood and living plants, eventually to mature and emerge into flying adults often towards dusk.

As leaves grow tired in the summer heat, hedgerows can lose the vivid green of springtime, fading now to russet. The leaves of tall Horse Chestnut trees stressed by heat and dryness brown at the margins. Desiccated tresses formerly bearing the fine seeds and down of willows also fall to the ground, their purposes served and their nutrients returning to fertilise the soils from which the next generations of willows will sprout.

In all of this brownness, there is diversity, from fawn and tan to ochre, buff and into blackness. Life proceeds in profusion into the driest part of the years, in fifty and many more shades of brown and all grades between.

NATURE'S ECOLOGICAL ECONOMY

THE STAGGERING VARIETY of life in rainforests, savannah or coral reefs impresses. So too does that in an everyday garden lawn like ours: a typical patch that is neither 'bowling green' nor unkempt tundra in which one would be unsurprised to stumble across Shergar or the lost city Atlantis. In a few square inches are Daisy, Bugle, Eyebright, Ribwort, Cowslip, Dove's-foot Cranesbill, Hawksbeard, White Clover, Dandelion, Hawksbeard, Ryegrass and other grasses too mown to identify. And that's before looking closer at fine mosses or getting out the microscope to see beyond those.

Riparian meadows are even more diverse, comprising grasses such as *Briza*, *Lolium*, *Festuca*, *Holcus* and *Alopecurus*, and herbs like Red and

White Clovers, Black Medick, Dock, Stinging Nettle, Cow Parsley and
Common Hogweed, Teasel and Burdock to name just a few. Riverside
trees include Crack Willow, Sallow, White Willow and Osier, Ash, Alder,
Hawthorn, Elder, Hazel, Oak amongst others. Aquatic vegetation segues
from submerged milfoils and starworts, floating-leaved Yellow Water Lilies
and *Potamogetons*, emergent Reed Sweet-grass, Reed Canary Grass and
Arrowhead, and riparian stands of Purple Loosestrife, Hairy and Lesser
Willow-herbs, Stinging Nettle, Hemlock and Comfrey.

Predatory Pike, Perch and Eels, omnivorous Chub, Barbel, Dace and
Roach, and surface-feeding Brown Trout, Grayling and Bleak swim our
rivers, stream margins hosting smaller Minnows, Three-spined Sticklebacks,
Gudgeon, Stone Loach and Bullheads, each with a particular niche that
changes as sediment erodes or accretes in a magic carpet of ever-morphing river
habitats. Were we to explore the myriad minute or hidden life forms beyond
the acuity of our naked eyes, this would dwarf visible biodiversity many times
over.

Why doesn't nature make do with a singular generic grass, tree, water
plant, fish or insect? After all, don't they do pretty much the same things?

This simplistic view is how we run our economy. Most management
consultants espouse 'efficiency' as a mantra, eliminating redundant, parochial
or duplicate labour or facilities and other 'superfluous' costs, assuming stable
markets, policy frameworks and operating environments. Why should
ecosystems differ?

The answer lies in false assumptions about stability. No day, season or
year is the same meteorologically, no summer or winter equally cold or hot
or long, no rainfall regime guaranteed, even before we factor in changes in
climate both natural and human-induced. Nature is diverse precisely because
in diversity there is resilience, different pathways for recycling chemicals
and energy favoured by ever-changing conditions. Environmental extremes
maintain biodiversity, encoding nature's capacity for efficient functioning come
what may.

Conversely, contemporary markets see diversity as wastage and
inefficiency. Have we learned nothing from repeated economic and other
'shocks', big banks and other enterprises 'too big to fail', the economic
ramifications of tsunamis or extreme flood and droughts, uncertainties
wrought by political regime shifts nationally and internationally? Our
globalised economy is anything but stable, yet it is dominated substantially

by large, multinational quasi-monopolies that squeeze out the local and the diverse. Yet businesses and other institutions ultimately succeed or fail according to their capacities to adapt, not through inflexible 'efficiencies'.

We can learn much from river life and the rest of the natural world. Were we more like nature, adaptive and diverse in the way we organise our public services and businesses, rather than narrowly obsessed with least cost in the shorter term that generally favours centralisation and the wealthy minority whilst marginalising the rest, perhaps we too could better ride out the fluctuations in an economic environment as volatile as the natural and human worlds that shape it.

In nature, the term 'richness' is almost synonymous with diversity; why should we regard economic richness in a totally different, myopic light?

AUGUST

THE WATER SNAKE

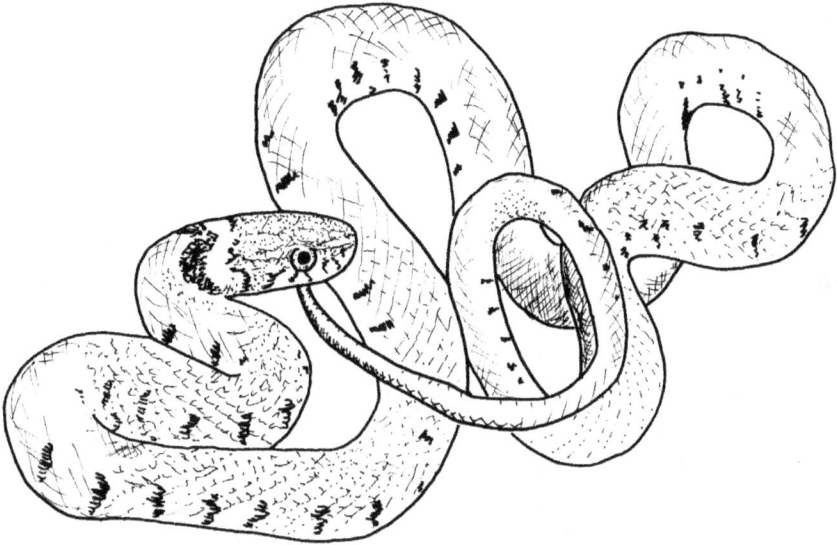

ONE OF SUMMER'S more thrilling sights is the sinuous weave of a Grass Snake (*Natrix natrix*) swimming across the river's surface. Grass Snakes are capable swimmers, not only crossing between banks on the surface but also hunting underwater for amphibians, small fishes and other aquatic prey. So strong is the affinity of the Grass Snake with water that it is also known as the 'Water Snake', as well as the 'Ringed Snake' after the distinctive yellow or pale cream collar behind the head. The Latin name 'Natrix' is also derived from 'nare' or 'natare', meaning 'to swim'.

Grass Snakes are handsome beasts, the largest of Britain's snakes with a base colour generally of dull green but varying from khaki to grey or black. In common with many reptiles, darker colours are more frequent in cooler climates and at higher altitudes, better adapting them for efficient absorption of heat from weaker sunlight. As ectothermal ('cold-blooded') animals, Grass Snakes bask in sunlight to raise their body temperatures enabling them to become active.

Typically in late March, male Grass Snakes emerge from hibernation, generally in log piles, leaf litter or other insulated crevices, spending much of suitable days basking in sunlight to raise their body temperatures encouraging

maturation of sperm. Female Grass Snakes, longer than males at up to one
metre, emerge around a fortnight later, generally in early April depending on
weather. The more active males immediately descend upon emerging females
to mate. Leathery-skinned eggs are laid in warm, rotting vegetation, including
leaf piles and compost heaps. Tiny snakes, around eighteen centimetres long,
hatch from them after six or eight weeks.

But not everyone welcomes the sight of a grass snake. Whilst rational
evolutionary factors might explain aversion to snakes in general, it is beyond
my comprehension why so many people in our village said they were pleased
that a big female Grass Snake was found run over and killed in the main
street some years ago. Grass Snakes are entirely harmless and non-venomous,
feeding substantially on amphibians as well as hunting efficiently for small
fishes and a range of other smaller animals. Every year, at least once, Grass
Snakes visit our garden ponds and take every last newt, though our profuse
smooth newt population rebounds immediately.

Grass Snakes occur across Europe from Scandinavia down to Southern
Italy, across the Middle East and into Northern Africa. They are one of three
snake species in Britain, the island of Ireland remaining famously snake-free.
The extremely rare Smooth Snake (*Coronella austriaca*) is also non-venomous,
confined now to a few scattered sites across southern England. The Adder
(*Vipera berus*), also known as the Viper, is widespread. It is the only venomous
snake in Britain, though it is not aggressive and has a small mouth so there
is little to fear from an Adder, less commonly seen near water, with human
fatalities almost vanishingly rare and most bites resulting from the snake
defending itself from unwise handling. Unlike the Grass Snake, female
Smooth Snakes and Adders retain fertilised eggs within their bodies, giving
birth to active young. All of these snakes suffer from 'bad press', posing no or
at best minuscule risk to people and pets.

Like many river-lovers, I welcome the 'Water Snake' on warm summer
days when I chance upon one sunning itself, hunting the bank or insinuating
its way between Yellow Water Lily pads on the languid river's surface.
Sharing the river with such imposing wild creatures is, after all, a principal
element of our enjoyment of fishing, walking, picnicking or otherwise
spending time within the magical tapestry of the river valley.

THE HORSE STINGER

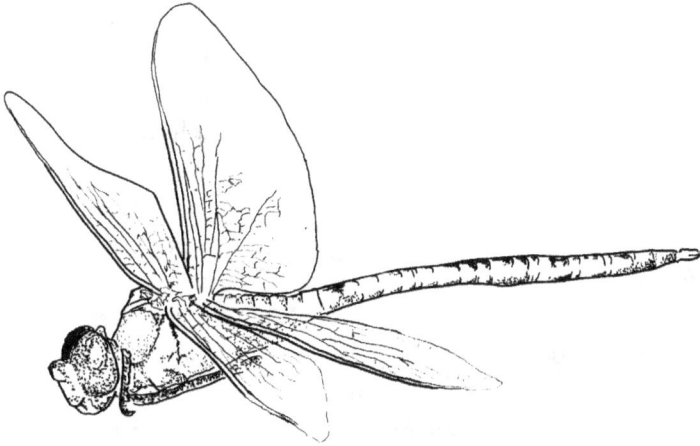

A N INTERESTING THING about the horse stinger is that it doesn't sting horses. Not only does it lack stinging parts, it also has no interest in horses.

Another interesting thing about the horse stinger – the name's origin is lost in history – is that it is also known as the devil's darning needle. It is of no use as a darning needle, and this is not the place for metaphysical discussion about the devil's existence.

We know these impressive acrobats of waterways and fields as dragonflies. Britain's dragonflies come in varied sizes, shapes and hues from the mighty Emperor Dragonfly (*Anax imperator*), or Blue Emperor, with a body length of over three inches to several smaller hawker dragonflies, stubby-bodied chasers, skimmers with their tapered bodies and several species of shorter darters amongst which the Ruddy Darter (*Sympetrum sanguineum*) is most common and also perhaps the most striking as the male's body can be blood-red.

Dragonflies are closely related to the smaller damselflies, which differ by having smaller eyes with a clear gap between them, narrow twig-like bodies, two pairs of wings of the same size that are held erect above backs at rest unlike dragonflies that have different-shaped fore and hind wings and spread them outwards like an aeroplane. The damselflies are equally fascinating, deserving separate discussion of their own.

Most dragonflies emerge on the wing in summer in a complex life cycle of three discrete phases – egg, larva and adult (lacking a pupal stage) – all dependent on rivers and pools.

Female dragonflies potentially lay hundreds of eggs in batches over a period of days or weeks, inserted into plant material, rotting organic matter or mud below or close to the water's surface or else deposited into water as the female insect dips her abdomen into the water whilst hovering. The exact egg-laying behaviour varies between species.

Mainly, the eggs hatch after between two and five weeks, though some hawkers and darters have overwintering eggs. Emerging larvae moult rapidly, predating other small animals and moulting many times over a period of one, two or more years depending on species and climate. Larval size, shape and life habits vary substantially between species.

Emergence of adult dragonflies from their larval skin is a thing of wonder. Moving first into water margins, the larvae climb up robust emergent stems. Then, by transferring body fluids, the adult insect bursts out of the drying skin over a period of around three hours. A dragonfly's first flight, yet to develop its final body colour, is tenuous. However, once the wings harden, the dragonfly is an agile flier feeding on flying insects and developing its mature colours before returning to the water to seek mates. Some species are markedly territorial. In some dragonflies, including the Emperor, the wings can audibly clatter when flying.

Egg-laying occurs soon after mating, in some species the female doing so alone whilst in others the male guard the female during laying. Life expectancy of adult dragonflies typically spans no more than a week or two, though can be up to eight weeks in some species.

Legends about dragonflies abound across the world, many associated with metamorphosis of consciousness. The common name 'dragonfly' is said to derive from them having once been dragons. The insect order comprising the dragonflies and damselflies is *Odonata*, derived from the Greek word 'odontes' meaning 'teeth' as these winged wonders were believed to have teeth though in fact they are toothless.

But facts can be stranger than fiction: *Meganeura* were long-extinct predatory insects from the Carboniferous period (300 million years ago) resembling and related to dragonflies but with wingspans of up to 70 centimetres (28 inches)!

WHOSE RIVER?

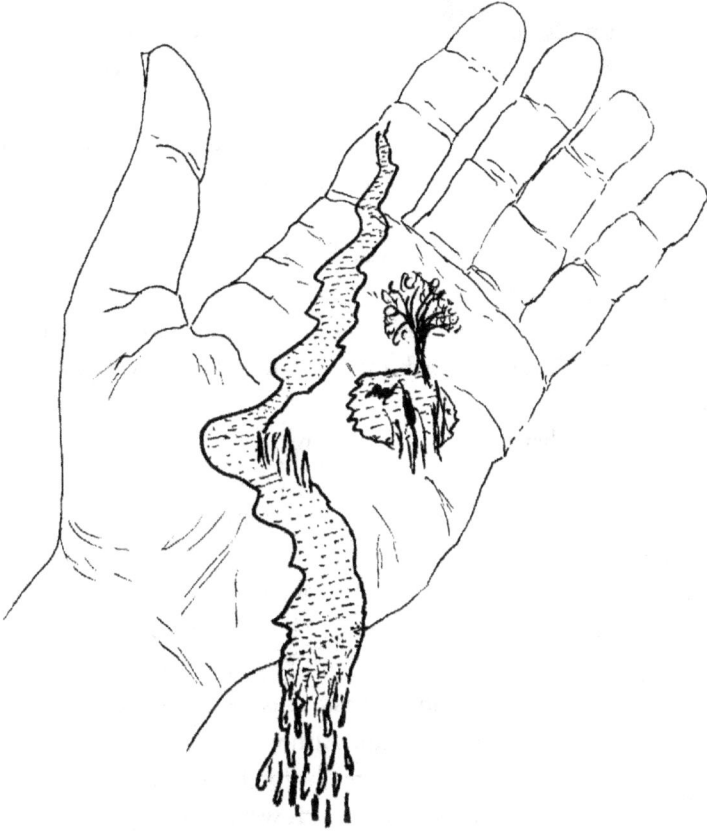

WE ALL ENJOY the river whether directly (fishing, walking, paddling or nature-watching) or indirectly through its profound influence on local character, real estate values, microclimate, soils and many other ways. In that sense, it is our river: a core defining and implicitly valued element of our shared home landscape.

However, from a narrower legal perspective, rivers are subject to various rights that limit or legitimise access.

Owners of riverside land have riparian rights, but also responsibilities. Owners have rights to protect their land from erosion and flood damage conditional to legal consents but, amongst other obligations, have a duty to ensure that water passes undiminished in quantity and quality.

Sporting and property rights are different beasts. Though often both held by riparian owners, these rights are also frequently owned separately. A fishing club or association, for example, may own fishing rights on the banks of one or more fields, without owning the land itself. This divergence of rights ownership can emerge as something of a surprise where people purchase riverside property, particularly on high-value fisheries such as Hampshire's River Test, discovering only later that they not only hold no fishing or other sporting rights but are obliged to permit unfettered access to those that do.

Ownership of the river bed varies. Land bounded by a watercourse is generally assumed to include ownership of the bed out to mid-channel, unless the bed is explicitly owned by someone else (as is often the case for artificial watercourses) or the property deeds mark a wall or hedge as the owner's boundary.

Navigation rights differ again, sometimes held by public bodies though many rivers have none, and nor is there any implicit 'Right to Roam'.

All these rights can be leased out. Local clubs commonly lease fishing rights from farmers and other land-owners, in the same way that people lease the physical property of riparian farmland or gardens.

Whatever the riparian and sporting rights, the water itself is owned by the state, and is therefore in theory owned by all of us. Use of the water for abstraction and disposal of liquid waste must be licensed through the Environment Agency (in England). Although riparian rights allow withdrawal of a limited amount of water, beyond a minimal level it is necessary to obtain an abstraction licence. However, riparian rights do not permit disposal of waste matter, which can only be done under licence.

Wildlife associated with the river is subject to a whole different set of rights, legally generally constituting *ferae naturae* – literally 'wild nature' – owned by all and none of us. If a landowner or fishing club buys then stocks fish into a river, the fish immediately become *ferae naturae* once released. An exception is in fully enclosed still waters, in which case they may be owned. However, whilst the fish in a river may not be owned, sporting rights to fish for them generally are.

Superimposed on this complex matrix of property and other rights is centuries of case law establishing precedents over contested rights from the time of the Byzantine emperor Justinian I early in the 6th century AD. 'Justinian law', evolving into the contemporary British system of Common

Law, is replicated across many countries (particularly those we formerly invaded!)

The river and wider catchment provides water for our domestic, industrial, agricultural and other needs, maintains biodiversity and its many societal benefits ranging from pollination to natural beauty and spiritual inspiration. It supports our food needs too, both harvested and cultured, also stabilising the global climate and moderating the local climate. The river characterises our landscape, supports diverse recreational and other cultural uses, boosts local property values and enriches our lives in many other tangible and less tangible ways.

Rivers then transcend boundaries of geography and possession, as indeed those of time and generations. River are not merely something owned or to which human rights are natural. They are a legacy from the past and a bequest for the future, axial not only for us transient humans but to the myriad species sharing this Earth as well as their evolutionary heritage and future.

So whose is the river?

Yours, mine, our forebears and descendants: at once none and all of us. What is clear though is that what we really own is a duty of care to ensure that, like riparian responsibilities for the water it carries, the river and its many gifts flow undiminished in quantity and quality into the future.

WHAT'S THE POINT OF WASPS?

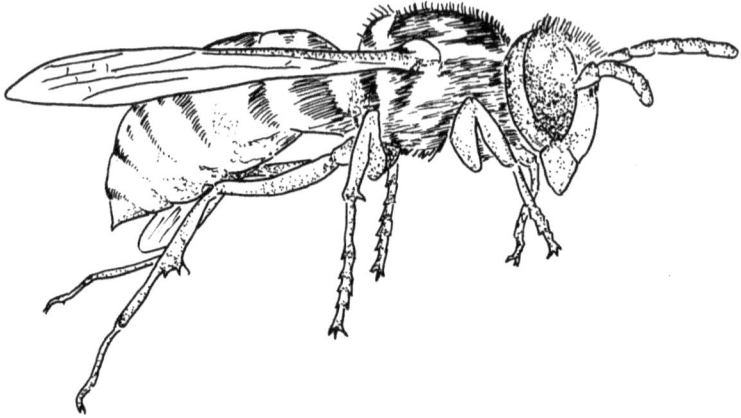

As I'm always banging on about the values of nature, I'm also sometimes asked about the purpose of slugs, microbes and other ostensibly unappealing beasties.

In the midst of the English summer, it is perhaps timely to address the not infrequently raised query "*What's the point of wasps?*" Few, it seems, have deep affection for these buzzy, stingy, picnic-raiding beasties, so here are a few thoughts.

Firstly, wasps are inherently fascinating. There are over 100,000 wasp species globally with more being discovered. Most are brilliantly adapted predators or parasites; almost every insect pest species having at least one species of wasp that preys on or parasitizes it.

All nine of the familiar yellow-and-black banded British species belong to a subset of wasps in which the ovipositor (egg-laying appendage) is modified into a venomous sting. This subset is also known as the 'paper wasps', as they build intricate and water-resistant grey or brown papery nests from chewed fibres from dead wood and plant stems mixed with saliva.

Wasps also have fascinating social structures. In spring, large queen wasps emerge from hibernation to found a colony and start building a new nest from which they never again emerge. Her eggs produce the sterile worker wasps commonly encountered in gardens and picnics in increasing numbers as spring and summer progresses, whose roles include hunting small, mainly insect prey incapacitated with the sting and carried back to the ever-growing nest to feed larvae tended by other sterile workers.

The predatory and parasitic activities of wasps control populations of prey insects, which would otherwise proliferate producing escalating crop damage and loss and/or greater reliance on damaging pesticides and other management interventions. Some wasps also feed on pollen, providing pollination services.

Wasps serve as important links in food chains, both as they die and are re-absorbed into ecosystems but also because a surprisingly diversity of organisms eat wasps. Invertebrates preying on wasps include several species of dragonflies, robber flies and hoverflies, and some other wasps, beetles and moths. Various vertebrates also feed on wasps, including numerous species of birds (133 bird species just in the Western Palearctic consume wasps at least occasionally) and also badgers, bats, weasels, rats and mice and, overseas, animals such as wolverines. Older anglers will know that wasp grubs (larvae) are an effective bait for many coarse fish species. Furthermore, some people eat wasps, typically as grubs which are reportedly quite tasty.

Wasps thereby play significant roles in species balances and natural cycles of productivity, nutrients and energy. The activities of wasps are consequently of significant value to farmers, foresters, horticulturalists and gardeners, and all who benefit from their produce. These contributions are ever-more important given emerging concerns about global food and resource security and the need to reduce dependence on harmful synthetic substances. Further economic activities related to wasps include markets for nest removal, nest-destroying chemicals, swatters and wasp deterrents, and let us not forget markets for antihistamine and other treatments for wasp stings.

Wasps have also inspired artistic expression, including Ralph Vaughan Williams incidental music "*The Wasps*" (written in 1909 for a production of Aristophanes' *The Wasps*) and also a fictional superheroine character called 'Wasp' published in Marvel Comics books from 1963. Some 'art forms' attributed to the real or imagined characteristics of wasps are more literal and edifying than others!

This is not the final word on all that wasps do for us, but it is a good first step towards addressing the question "*What's the point of wasps?*" All in all, there is quite a big point to wasps, and I'm not just talking about the big stingy thing at their rear ends!

FEAST AND FAMINE

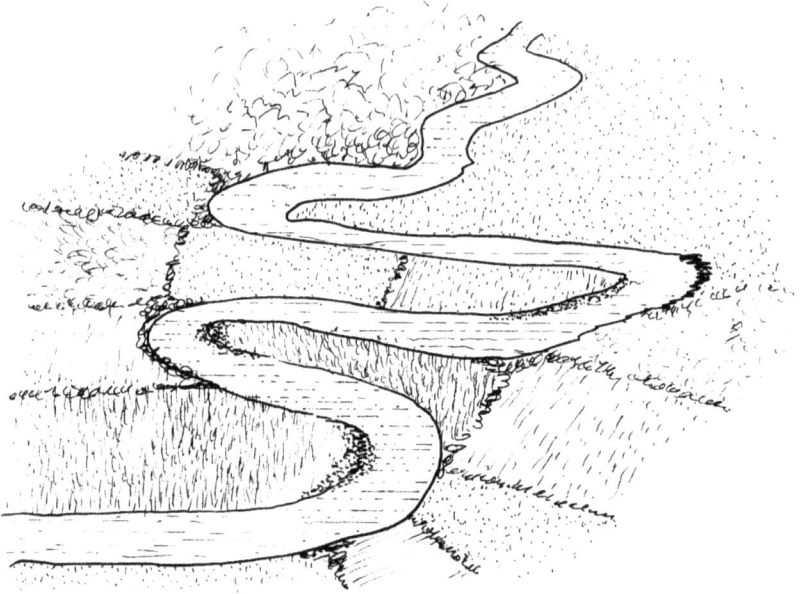

M Y LOCAL RIVER has been recognised as a sickly beast since the early 1990s. Specifically, low flows in headwaters have seen upper catchment tributaries classified amongst the nation's priority 'low flow' rivers. Partly, this is consequent from their being substantially fed from groundwater, the slow passage of water through permeable limestone strata percolating to the surface in springs the discharge of which waxes and wanes with varying depth of the water table. But we have significantly compounded this natural variability. This is an increasingly common situation the length and breadth of the land.

Groundwater may be out of sight and out of mind below the feet, but when we turn on the tap or flush the cistern it is commonly groundwater we tap into in many regions of the country. The demands of our dense population place growing stresses on surface and underground water resources alike. A big difference between these sources though is that we have far from complete knowledge about the places and rates at which groundwater systems, or aquifers, are replenished, and the contributions they make to streams, pools, wetlands and general soil moisture over very broad landscapes.

We also have to factor in the many things we do that impede percolation of rainfall into groundwater, inhibiting its replenishment. Urban 'hard' infrastructure such as paving, roofs, asphalt and car parks prevent free passage of water through soil into underground rock strata. Run-off surges over these surfaces during rainfall, picking up all manner of contaminants ranging from oils, rubber, metals, dust and other substances, concentrated pulses causing urban flooding and pollution.

Rural areas too are problematic. Clearance of natural permeable habitat, such as forests and wetlands, inhibits groundwater recharge. Heavy machinery on tilled land can 'pan' the soil, compacting surface layers particularly whilst the soil is damp. Digging down through compacted soil even in wet conditions can reveal layers not far below the surface that are bone dry. Overstocking with animals also compacts soil surfaces with similar consequences for permeability. 'Muddy floods' of surface run-off, eroding soil and carrying with it other microbial and chemical contaminants, rob aquifers and compound flood and pollution problems.

Market forces and legacy regulations combine to desiccate landscapes, some 90% of our natural heritage of wetlands lost since Roman times. Consequently, we suffer a 'feast and famine' of water veering from flood to drought, and sometimes both simultaneously as excess surface water fails to refill groundwater sources exploited for public supply.

Some suggest we should build more dams in headwaters, capturing water from strong flows for use in drier times. But this is narrow thinking. Water is more than a physical commodity to be warehoused for our utility. A dam is not a lake, just as a pipe, canal or conveyance channel is not a vibrant, living river ecosystem producing a wealth of benefits to all in society. Many cultures know this, particularly in arid and semi-arid lands, imbuing water with spiritual and symbolic qualities that we tend largely to dismiss. Yet water is at the heart of living systems: nourishing, connecting, conveying, fertilising, cleansing, scouring, cooling, nurturing.

We need to welcome water once again into landscapes we have massively drained and made impermeable through historic development. Though benefits from historic agricultural intensification and urban sprawl are significant, within contemporary practices are the seeds of their own limitation as we struggle with the threats of both water shortage and flood, lost biodiversity, depleted soil carbon and fertility, erosion and fishery degradation. We need to relearn our lost water wisdoms, 'farming' landscapes as much for water and wildlife as for commodities, supported by appropriate rewards and sanctions reflecting implications for public wellbeing. And we need our towns and cities to become more permeable, allowing water to seep downward through managed greenery that also purifies air, pleases aesthetically and, not insignificantly, also improves real estate values.

Our complicity in today's feast and famine of water needs to be banished to history as we relearn the value of the roles landscapes play in storing, purifying and buffering flows both above and below ground, together with the many life-sustaining and enriching contributions that restoring nature's much-degraded natural processes can confer upon us.

SEPTEMBER

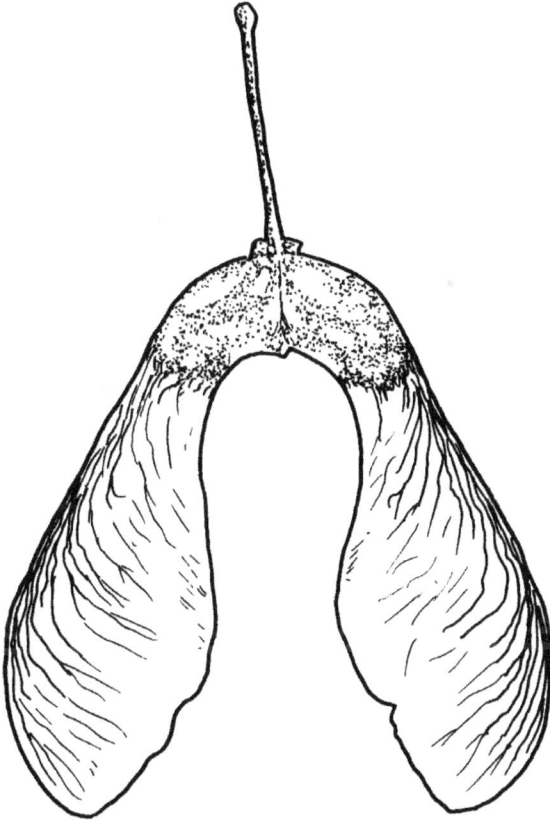

A PROLIFERATION OF FISHES

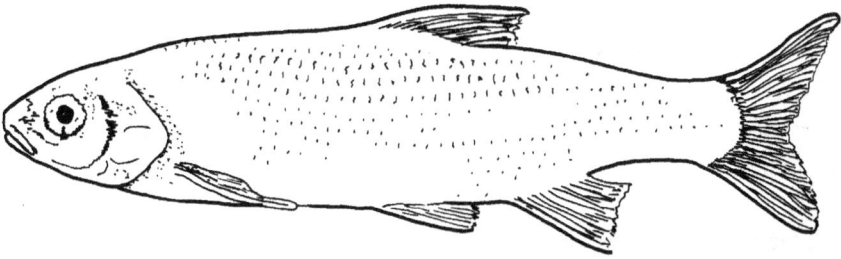

YOU MAY OR may not noticed that, sometimes in late summer, rivers can seem to be positively heaving with little fishes. Not just the Minnows and other 'tiddler' species, about which I have waxed enthusiastically on TV and radio. No, this time I am talking about thriving populations of the juveniles of larger fish species such as Dace (*Leuciscus leuciscus*), Chub (*Squalius cephalus*) and Roach (*Rutilus rutilus*), all about a hand's width long. So what is the reason for such a rich, seasonal profusion?

To answer this, we have to recognise that these 'silver fish' species are generally long-lived, Roach and Dace potentially reaching a good age of twelve to fourteen years whilst Chub can live for more than twenty years. So they are subject to cumulative, multi-year pressures.

The severity of winter conditions during exceedingly cold years – in particular shortages of food and increased predation particularly by Cormorants and other major predators abandoning larger still water that may have frozen over – can exert a 'double whammy' impact. Firstly, direct mortality of many larger fish is not uncommon as deep cold bites into the river imposing a range of stresses. Secondly, for surviving female fish, there is much-reduced deposition of yolk into eggs developing during the winter in preparation for spawning in spring or early summer the following year.

Survival of juvenile fish is also subject to multi-year effects, particularly so for Chub which require higher temperatures for spawning often doing so over river gravels in early summer. Fry growth to sufficient size and strength commonly limits their ability to survive spates during their first autumn and winter. This is affected primarily by four factors: sufficient small food items; river margins rising during summer days to as much as 10°C warmer than water in the channel; shelter from currents as larval fish when first free-swimming are about the size of a human eyelash and have incompletely developed muscles and fins; and, finally, sufficient yolk content in the eggs to provide a 'kick start' to early growth.

So fry survival in their first winter is directly related both to conditions the previous winter as well as during the summer after hatching. This is why management of river habitat, particularly provision of suitable marginal 'nursery' habitat, is such an important consideration in rivers that are often today simplified in structure both by development and also farming pressures such as grazing and tillage right up to the banks. An increasing number of habitat improvement measures are now being put in place across Britain, reversing a former management paradigm of 'sanitising' the river edge, for the purpose of improving fry and older fish refuge, food availability and breeding places.

Putting these jigsaw pieces together, the juvenile fish abounding in our river right now have benefitted from successive recent warmer winters and summers with relatively few severe spates. This is compounded by a relative paucity of larger fish due to previous severe winters, relieving predation on eggs and fry as well as competition for food. Also, positive river habitat management seems to be resulting in beneficial outcomes for the regeneration of fish populations, and with them the wider health of the river and its natural complement of wildlife.

Next time you walk by the river, just stop a moment to watch and to enjoy this natural abundance!

SLEEPING IN THE
RIVER MUD

NIGHTS DRAW IN and cool mists hug the river valley that much longer at dawn and dusk with the coming of September.

Swallows (*Hirundo rustica*) and House Martins (*Delichon urbicum*) know this. Some adult birds may already have departed. Younger birds from later broods linger until later in the season, some perhaps into October, before obeying the call of the flyway to southern Africa.

Waves of birds mass before departure – I have seen them do so in South Africa before heading northwards as well as across Europe before heading south – generally forming dense squadrons over open water and wetlands to feed up on emerging insects as fuel for the trials ahead.

Then, they are gone, their bustle suddenly conspicuous by its absence from the chilling landscape. And as suddenly, they reappear in the opposite hemisphere, once again massing over and near water to feast on emerging insects in order to recharge and regenerate bodies spent on the rigours of an incredible journey of up to seven thousand miles.

Centuries ago, given prevalent knowledge and narrower world views, it was not such a massive intuitive leap for people to believe that these birds hibernated in the mud of rivers and lakes. After all, that is the place where they massed before suddenly vanishing in the fall, only to reappear in these same locations in April.

We take our contemporary knowledge as a given, perhaps even sniggering at the ignorance of our forebears. Would that we actually acted proportionately upon our rich legacy of knowledge, rather than living lifestyles that on even cursory examination are unsustainable to the extent of threatening future security let alone the potential for equity across society. But that's a rant for another day!

So, given the facts and the perspectives of the day, the notion of these summertime visitors sleeping the winter through in river mud is not such a mad idea. After all, that's what a lot of seeds, amphibians, insect larvae and even some fish do.

So we all now know that they migrate annually *en masse* between northern and southern temperate zones. But is this also true, or just hearsay from our current accepted world view?

In fact, the window of migration southwards from our shores can run from mid-August through until quite late in the year, laggards often driven by increasingly unstable weather as much as the pull from the antipodes. They also do so in dribs and drabs, rather than as a population. Not only that, the autumn migration can be rather protracted as birds often move only short distances every few days to roosts at a lower latitude. Swallows milling over and around your home today may well not be those nesting locally all summer, but could have arrived from Scotland, northern England or Ireland as 'our' birds departed further south.

So the reverse pattern occurs in spring, right? Well, not really. The spring migration is a far more condensed affair as it is essential for birds to get to their destination expeditiously, particularly due to substantial competition amongst males to secure a mate and suitable nesting site. The spring migration from South Africa to our shores can take about five weeks, during which these slight birds miraculously cover about 300 kilometres each day. (That's 186 miles: about the same distance between London and Swansea.) No wonder they mass to feed so intensively on emerging insects, which serve as vital 'power packs' for the journey and for recovery thereafter.

So that is that mystery solved. Or is it?

Well, we also now know that some Swallows, albeit a substantial minority, winter in various locations in between their breeding territories and traditional southern hemisphere wintering strongholds. Many do so in northern Africa and eastern Mediterranean countries, some stragglers even remaining within southern Europe, particularly southern Spain. Increasing numbers are now recorded overwintering as far north as Britain and Ireland, most likely prompted by our changing climate.

So wave a fond farewell to the straggling House Martins and Swallows before they venture south to evade the clutches of the coming winter, safe in the knowledge that, like the spring blooms and Cuckoo, they will return to us in the coming spring. Also pause a moment to reflect on what we know, and what we think we know but may merely assume unquestioningly. Then, the former notion of these birds sleeping the winter through in the river mud may not seem so crazy after all.

COMMON WILLOWS

O NE OF THE most prominent trees marching along our river banks is
the Crack Willow (*Salix fragilis*), marking the channel's winding path.
Viewed from an aeroplane, it is hard to discern a river by its water. But the
meandering trace of willows is a giveaway.

The Crack Willow is one of Britain's largest native willows, reaching 25
metres. It is widely distributed across Europe and Western Asia, particularly
beside watercourses and pools. The characteristically deeply fissured bark of
an older willow, as well as its fine twigs and slender, oval leaves, are familiar
sights in both rural and urban areas. Indeed, it is such a common presence that
we are perhaps over-familiar with the tree and its remarkable properties.

The name 'Crack Willow' derives from the tendency of the wood to
split with an audible 'crack'. Fallen trunks and dislodged twigs and branches
readily root, regenerating like some wooden version of Dr Who into new, fast-
growing shoots. Twigs can be carried by water some distance, representing a
remarkably efficient dispersal strategy.

Willow saplings and the mighty trees that grow from them play a major
role in stabilising river banks. Without them, and water-loving Alder trees

and other willow species, our rivers would be far less stable and so prone to erode banks.

Willows also play host to a variety of riverside birds. Boughs leaning over water provide perches for Kingfishers to prey on fish, many smaller birds perching and nesting in them and Sparrowhawks often launching raids from within their cover. There is also a mutually beneficial relationship between bees and some other insects, food exchanged for fertilisation of willow flowers. Various willow species feed a wide diversity of other insects including the caterpillars of the Puss Moth, Eyed Hawk-moth and Red Underwing moth amongst many more.

Submerged willow roots offer valuable spawning, nursery, feeding, refuge and ambush habitat for fish. I have taken underwater photographs around submerged willow roots from the Bristol Avon that rival the grandest coral reefs in terms of the wealth of fish life crowding around and within their protective maze.

But willows do far more things for us than that. They absorb much of the energy of storms sweeping the landscape, sheltering stock and averting damage to crops and property. All species of willow have cultural significance going back through recorded history. They are referred to in poetry, including Shakespeare's Hamlet, in traditional dances such as 'stripping the willow', and on ceremonial occasions substituting for palm branches to celebrate Palm Sunday in northern regions.

Slender willow shoots are used for basket-weaving, manufacture of fish traps, wattle fences, wattle and daub house walls which were often woven from willow shoots, traditional Welsh boats known as coracles, and wicker ware which has a long history and many applications. The willow wood was used to manufacture brooms, boxes, furniture, toys and musical instruments and a host of other products. Extracts of willow were used for tanning, as fibre, and as a constituent of paper, rope and string, and for the manufacture of charcoal. Cricket Bat Willow, a hybrid of White Willow and Crack Willow, is used, as the name suggests, for the manufacture of cricket bats. Today, willow is now often grown as a biofuel owing to its fast growth rate, and willows also serve as effective media in constructed wetlands for wastewater treatment and remediation of contaminated land.

There are many more direct uses of willows, including the various uses of willow products in traditional medicines. The leaves and bark of the willow tree are referred to in ancient texts from Assyria, Sumer and Egypt as a remedy for rheumatic aches and fever. Hippocrates, the Ancient Greek physician, wrote about the diverse medicinal properties of willows in the fifth century BC, whilst willow has also been a staple medicinal treatment of Native Americans. As previously noted, willows also produce a precursor of aspirin, the first 'wonder drug' of the modern era which came into production in 1897 giving rise subsequently to a hugely important class of drugs known as nonsteroidal anti-inflammatory drugs (NSAIDs).

The Crack Willow is but one of many willow species found in our shores – also including Sallow (Goat Willow), Osier, White Willow, Grey Willow and many more – part of the well over 300 species and many more hybrids known worldwide.

From their diverse significant roles in ecosystems to their ceremonial, utilitarian, medicinal and structural values, not to mention their contribution to landscapes prized by people, there is nothing 'common' about the common willow tree. Without them, whether or not you are a 'tree hugger', our lives would be immensely poorer, not to mention more vulnerable.

JEWELS IN THE LANDSCAPE

DURING THE PROLONGED biting cold of winter 1996/7, excoriating
northerly winds whipped temperatures down as low as -12°C in my
back garden. I don't recall much snow, but the ground, garden ponds and
water butt were frozen hard as iron and fish in the ice-fringed river lay
torpid.

In those days, I used to take 'time off' rather more seriously. So, with
fishing to any practical purpose off the agenda, what was a riverwatcher to do?
I unfolded my Landranger map, donned walking boots (hard-frozen ground
rendering wellingtons unnecessary) and strode into the chill winds to visit each
of the little blue dots in the parish.

Ponds, no matter how seemingly insignificant, are a particular passion.
Each is distinct, uniquely influenced by the countryside and land uses, shading
and depth, runoff and groundwater inputs, extent of trampling by livestock
and diverse other influences. One is just not sure what one will find. In
their season, they host unusual and sometimes rare animals and plants, often

quite different to those in the adjacent river, as well as nesting birds, visiting mammals and all manner of other mysteries.

As a kid in the dawn of the 1960s, the Kentish countryside accessible to my little legs was strewn with water bodies glistening pearlescent against Wealden pastureland and hop fields. Some held Three-spined Sticklebacks (*Gasterosteus aculeatus*), or occasionally larger fishes. Moorhens (*Gallinula chloropus*) were common, fanning out to exploit the diverse, often secluded wetland pockets in the landscape after overwintering communally on larger lakes and rivers. Commonly, Water Voles (*Arvicola terrestris*) bustled across open water. Other pools were swamp-like, choked with grasses and water weeds yet rife with Smooth and Great-crested Newts and their feathery-gilled larvae, Ramshorn, Great Pond and other water snails, and not infrequently visited by lithe Grass Snakes seeking amphibian prey. Dragonfly larvae and water beetles, water fleas and willows, grasses and pondweeds populated these small worlds in which I could, and still can, lose myself hour after hour. Some were depressions into which water drained, others were fed from springs upwelling from deeper subterranean strata, still more had been dug as dewponds to water livestock, and a good few began life as water-filled bomb craters from what then was quite recent history.

Alas, Britain lost around 90% of its ponds during the last century. Changing agricultural patterns were primary drivers, with no great incentive to retain ponds for farming purposes when better supplies of piped water were available and with economics and technology demanding bigger fields for more uniform energised management. Similar fates befell once abundant hedgerows and copses. The scattering of watery pearls in that Kentish landscape was already notably sparser by the late 1960s as the housing boom and a new bypass swamped many in my early childhood locale. The past six decades have been even less kind.

My informal familiarisation with the frozen north Wiltshire pondscape that cold winter, now over two decades ago, suggested a familiar litany of abandonment, infilling or ploughing over, or siltation and succession to wet scrub or even complete dry land. We would be ill-advised to let these pearls fade and die as, however tiny they may be, they form a constellation of wildlife reservoirs and landscape corridors. They support a disproportionately large complement of rare invertebrates, are a haven for amphibians, and host other scarce plants and animals including as a distributed network of vegetated nursery sites for breeding birds. Many ponds also have heritage importance, or serve as places for quiet refuge, learning, relaxation or sharing time.

We and nature need ponds, and ponds need us to care of them. So, pause a while when you encounter one of these much-neglected damp places. Watch a while and experience a precious, scattered fragment of wilderness in an otherwise busy landscape and world. Who knows, perhaps you will come to love it as your own secret 'special place'.

WATER BABIES

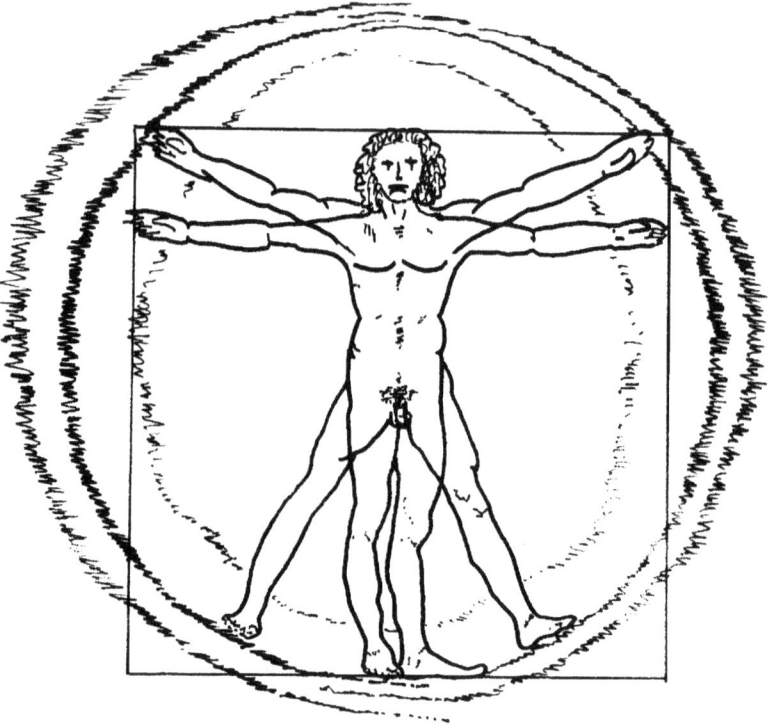

I T IS UNDENIABLY relaxing to spend time by water, be that a river, pool, the sea shore, a garden pond or a fish tank. The reasons for this are doubtless diverse, but maybe unsurprising when we consider our close kinship with that fluid element.

We were conceived in a water medium and were from that point largely water, a foetus comprising as much as 99% fluid. We develop structure from conception in an amniotic ocean, eventually born with soft bodies that may still comprise as much as 90% water. As adults, water accounts for more or less 65% of our mass, varying with body shape, sex and various other factors. If we are fortunate enough to achieve ossified old age, we lose water in proportion with muscle mass. An average 80-year-old holds 15% less water than a 20-year-old, but even then water still comprises some 55% of their weight.

Remaining well hydrated matters, requiring us to replenish anything from two-and-a-half to four litres of water every day through what we drink and eat. The movement of water in our bodies cools us as we sweat, conveys nourishment and oxygen to our cells, and bears away metabolic wastes for processing and elimination. We taste through substances dissolved in our mouths, and smells and odours are detected as they dissolve in the water film in our noses. Water buffers sensors in our inner ears enabling us to balance and to pick up vibrations collected by the outer ear and transmitted by the fine bones of the middle ear. Fluxes of soluble ions moving through water across nerve and brain cell membranes convey messages and process information subconsciously, also building consciousness.

Blocking natural flows of water into, around and out of us is a recipe for sickness. As a worst case, we die in a matter of around four days, varying with environmental conditions and health, if we are unable (or unwilling) to replenish our water content. Slower kidney functioning and loss of taste sensations as we age contribute to the fact that many older people may not realise that they could be chronically dehydrated.

The busy lives that many of us lead even in intervening years may also make us skimp on taking in sufficient water, and this is likely to be to our detriment. At whatever age, declining water content affects us adversely as a drier body may process the drugs we administer into it with far lower efficiency, as well as perform many other functions of great importance at less rapid pace. Dehydration may also dim our perceptions, our fleetness of foot and of thinking, suppressing concentration and ability to learn, and hampering many other vital processes affecting not merely our physical health but also our moods. Desiccation is a major contributor to our propensity to physical as well as mental disorders.

Water in the form of a fish tank in the dentist's waiting room, in the downtown shopping mall, as a feature in business parks and other engineered landscapes, in the Zen garden or in many other built settings is a conspicuous indicator of the importance accorded to proximity to water in our everyday lives.

Water heals, cools, dissolves, cleanses, conveys, transmits, cushions, lubricates, nurtures and serves so many functions in our bodies and minds, and throughout the wider natural world with which it also connects us. However else we conceive of ourselves, a major aspect of our identity is that we are an emanation of water in motion. We are, in short, water babies.

Is it any wonder then that we find relaxation and kinship when in proximity to the element that comprises such a dominant proportion of our mass, and is so crucial to our wellbeing?

OCTOBER

FALLING LEAVES

A UTUMN LEAVES ARE turning, adding golden majesty to the riverscape. The elongated leaves of Crack Willow tint yellow and brown, curl and fall. Those of the Hawthorn and Guelder-rose burnish too, their berries transmuting to fiery red. Alder leaves dry and tumble, exposing bare twigs and woody cones.

This is a time of change, the full days of lush greenery seguing sedately into winter. Much of the productivity of long, summer days is resorbed into the trunk, the function of leaves as collectors of solar energy now redundant. These foliar miracles of bioengineering then brown, wither and fall, often forming profuse carpets and mounds on the ground and the river bed. Little by little, they break down and vanish.

However, in their death they are anything but gone. Whereas the productivity of algae and submerged water plants contributes a significant proportion of available food in rivers and lakes naturally low in nutrient substances, on most chemically more enriched lowland rivers virtually all the productivity arrives from outside the channel. Instead, organic matter blowing, falling or washing into the river constitutes the base of most food chains. Those discarded leaves, along with other animal and plant matter, substantially drive the river's productivity.

River invertebrates are classified in many ways: taxonomically (crustaceans, insects, worms and so on); by habitat usage (benthic, planktonic, etc.); but often also by feeding guilds. A 'feeding guild' simply describes the adaptations of invertebrates to different diets.

One such feeding guild is the 'shredders': animals like freshwater shrimps that break down larger pieces of organic matter such as dead leaves. 'Grazers', such as many species of cased caddis larvae, harvest fine, loose organic matter from submerged surfaces. 'Scrapers', such as water snails, scrape it from hard surfaces. 'Filter feeders', such as blackfly larvae, filter fine particulate matter from suspension in the water column. Much of the energy content of their food derives directly or indirectly from dead leaves, just as the feeding guild of 'Predators' feeds on other animals nourished by these leaves. So, in turn, fishes, birds, mammals, reptiles and other organisms feeding both on river invertebrates and the other creatures that consume them are substantially nourished, through links in the food chain, by falling leaves.

Viewed closely, the hues and patterns of falling leaves are living art. Or perhaps they are just untidy. It depends, I guess, on your point of view.

However, each one is condensed sunlight. The alchemy of photosynthesis locks away energy captured from the sun's rays throughout the growing season, storing it in the chemical bonds of complex organic molecules. Each dead leaf is a time capsule of condensed summer goodness, unlocked little by little and recycled throughout the cold, dark months by complex river ecosystem.

Every dried, shed leaf is another everyday miracle of nature. Through its own death, discarded from the tree that formed it, it gives new life to the whole river and landscape that, in turn, sustains the trees that, long months ahead, will produce new greenery to harvest the strengthening sunlight of another summer as part of an endless cycle.

BUSY BEES

T HE PACE OF nature is slowing with the cooler days and longer nights, but still there is a bustle in the riverside vegetation. Though frosts will shortly claim their ephemeral lives, bees are prominent amongst this ever-busy micro-menagerie.

Aside from producing the honey from which their name derives, Honey Bees (*Apis mellifera*) are best known as pollinators. But in fact, the UK hosts around 250 bee species, only one of which is the familiar Honey Bee. There are 225 species of solitary bees, many in reality semi-communal tending to nest individually but close together in suitable habitat. These include 'Masonry Bees', found excavating burrows on warmer walls and dry banks in which they lay eggs and tend their developing grubs. Our islands also host 24 species of bumblebee, notably larger and covered with dense hair.

Virtually all bee species play roles in pollination, though bumblebees are far more effective than honey bees in pollination and setting of fruit in apple orchards. But bees are far from the only animals providing the vital service of pollination, without which nature would simply cease to function. Pollen

wasps, ants, a diversity of flies such as bee flies, sawflies and hoverflies, as well
as butterflies, moths and flower beetles also perform this service. Vertebrates
too can be important pollinators, not in the UK but elsewhere, including
bats and birds, some non-flying mammals such as monkeys and rodents, and
some lizards. Hummingbirds, honeyeaters and sunbirds, all with long beaks
adapted to sipping nectar, are some of the birds important globally in the
transfer of pollen from male flower parts to receptive female flower parts.

But back to our ever-busy bees. Unlike the annual nesting cycle of a
wasp, honey bee colonies comprising tens of thousands of individuals tend
to be perennial. There are both male and female honey bees. Biggest of all
are the egg-laying queens, which deposit eggs singly in waxy combs built by
worker bees. Workers too are female, but are non-reproducing and have their
ovipositors (egg-laying equipment) modified into a sting. The queen too can
sting. However, bees are less inclined to sting than the more aggressively
defensive wasps and hornets, and mainly do so when defending the nest from
attack or else when attacked or trodden on out of the nest. When fatally
injured, Honey Bees release a pheromone (hormone external to the body)
provoking other bees to attack and sting, overwhelming would-be aggressors
attacking their nest.

Workers, as the name suggests, labour tirelessly on behalf of the colony
collecting nectar, building cells, feeding the growing grubs, and defending and
cleaning the hive. Male bees – drones which lack a sting – are larger than
workers. They develop from unfertilised eggs, and have the singular duty of
finding and mating with a young 'virgin' queen.

Cells in which grubs of drones and new queens develop are larger than
those built for workers, and grubs that are to become queens also enjoy
differential feeding of 'royal jelly' secreted from glands in the hypopharynx
of worker bees. In fact, all bee grubs receive some royal jelly as they develop,
but the diet given to developing queens and drones is richer. Worker bees
raise a new queen generally when the existing queen ages or dies, or the
colony becomes excessively large. In the case of an over-large hive, the old
queen generally emerges from the hive a few days prior to the new queen
hatching, taking with her a swarm of roughly half the workers to establish
a new colony. If several virgin queens emerge at the same time, they signal
their location by emitting a high-pitched buzzing noise, known as 'piping', to
instigate a fight to the death with other virgin queens. The victor then scours
the hive for cells in which other queens are developing, stinging and killing

the grubs or pupae. At this point, the virgin queen then makes a nuptial flight outside of the hive, chased and mated by usually more than one competing drone. The mated queen returns to the hive and, from then on, is able to lay either fertilised or unfertilised eggs. Unfertilised eggs containing only half the full complement of chromosomes develop into drones, whilst fertilised eggs develop into either workers or virgin queens.

Whilst a queen may live for three to four years, drones usually die upon mating or are expelled from the hive before winter. Workers live for just a few weeks in the summer or slightly longer in the early part of a mild winter.

So if there's a buzzing in your hedgerow, or river bank, don't be alarmed now, but pause instead to appreciate the tireless labours these busy workers perform to their and our benefit, and their amazing life cycles.

SOUNDS OF THE
SEASONS

FOR ME, A habitual wanderer of river valleys in all seasons, there are two definitive sounds characterising each pole of the turning seasons.

The first of these sounds is the excited shriek of Swifts (*Apus apus*) as they cut the summer air on scythe-like wings during their so brief, fourteen-week sojourn within British shores to breed and then as rapidly depart. They arrive at some point in late April or May, announcing themselves with that ecstatic cry, meeting up with their partners – they mate for life – to nest communally in high gables, cliffs, hollow trees or similar inaccessible places. Then, later in the year, gregarious groups hawk the skies with that same joyous sound before then, as suddenly, departing our shores for warm foreign climes in Africa south of the Sahara where they follow the rains to take advantage of emerging insect populations.

My other definitive sound of the seasons is half-a-year away. Suddenly, one day in October, I hear the gregarious cackle of a flock of Fieldfares (*Turdus pilaris*) as they restlessly criss-cross the floodplain, scouring hedgerows for berries and seeds after their migratory flight from Scandinavia and beyond. Fieldfares are members of the thrush family, their English common name dating back to around the Eleventh Century and said to be derived from the Anglo-Saxon word 'Feldefare', meaning 'traveller through the fields'. During the summer months, Fieldfares breed in woodlands or scrub in northern Europe and Asia, and only exceptionally rarely in Britain. However, they head southwards to escape extremes of cold and food shortages during the winter, arriving in large numbers in Britain as well as venturing to other southern European countries and even down to the north Africa coast. The guttural flight and alarm calls of flocks of Fieldfares are, to me, the music of quiet river valleys once the trees shed their leaves, a music suddenly conspicuously absent towards the end of February or into March as these birds return in flocks to their summer quarters.

The latter half of September through into October is the interregnum. Swifts have departed, though straggling juvenile Swallows (*Hirundo rustica*) and House Martins (*Delichon urbicum*) still hawk the skies during shortening days. But the Fieldfares are not yet with us nor, if we have a late season, may they be for some weeks to come.

The riverscape is no less melodious. Remaining leaves on the tall Aspen trees (*Populus tremula*) still whisper as they tremble to the caress of the slightest breeze, at least until frosted nights hasten their fall. Kingfishers (*Alcedo atthis*) pipe their warning cries ever more stridently as mating territories revert to single occupancy for the coming colder months, and the young of the year are driven off mercilessly, many never to see a spring. Collared Doves (*Streptopelia decaocto*) coo over the sibilance of water rushing across the weir sill, the Tawny Owl (*Strix aluco*) crying out from tall trees to would-be mates as dusk encroaches.

But, for all the fanfare of river life, this is a moment of pause between the iconic sounds respectively of summer and winter that have thrilled me since childhood and, I am sure, will do so until I too flow to sea like the river.

I am sure that you also have found your own connections with specific instruments in the grand orchestra of nature. Long may they continue to enrich our lives, and we to care for them.

FLOODPLAIN FORAYS

A S YOU WANDER the floodplain, keep your eyes down as autumn is peak time for the emergence of mushrooms and other toadstools.

Field Mushrooms (*Agaricus campestris*) and larger Horse Mushrooms (*Agaricus arvensis*) are sought by keen forayers on floodplain fields, particularly those manured by cattle and horses. I recall one distant autumn gathering Field Mushrooms bigger than my frying pan, cooking them in slices like fungal steaks over the course of a few nights. Wild mushrooms have strong flavour and texture, knocking insipid commercial mushrooms into a metaphorical cocked hat. Many other edible fungi put in an autumnal appearance too. But recall that some are poisonous, a few deadly, and various are less flavoursome than dishcloths. The landowner's consent is required if you plan to take a few home.

Many myths surround toadstools, which loom large in art, literature and folklore. The appearance of rings of toadstools is cause for either joy or alarm. These 'Fairy Rings' are said to mark places where fairies come to dance after a rainstorm. But they are also associated with curses, of sleeping for 100 years or being whisked off to the land of the 'wee folk', should a person dare to enter such a ring. A legend from The Netherlands has it that fairy rings are where the Devil sets down his milk churn, with similarly strong if ungrounded associations with sorcery in other European countries. Prime amongst fungi with the greatest weight of legend is the charismatic Fly Agaric (*Amanita muscaria*), with its characteristic bright red top dotted with white and association with the roots of pine trees, perhaps related in some way to their toxic and hallucinogen properties. As many will know, they are not the only psychotropic toadstools found on our fields.

Fungi have many human uses ranging from direct consumption as food, to yeasts deployed in baking, brewing and cheese-making. Some are used as biological agents controlling bacterial and insect crop pests, reducing the need for pesticides and other toxic chemicals. The chemical activity of fungi is used in many ways, from sources of citric acid (vitamin C), penicillin and other antibiotics, statins, and in the manufacture of insulin and other human hormones.

Perhaps the most fascinating aspect of toadstools and mushrooms (there is no scientific distinction between the two terms) is that they are mere ephemeral manifestations of far larger organisms growing unseen and unappreciated under our feet. A visible toadstool is simply the fruiting body of a tangle of hyphae (fungal filaments) under the soil. The mycelium (network of hyphae) of many fungi form symbiotic relationships with the roots of higher plants, vital in making soil nutrients available to them. Others break down dead wood or other organic matter. Some mycelia (the plural of mycelium) may span many hectares (or acres if you prefer) and potentially be hundreds or even in some cases thousands of years old.

The visible fruiting bodies, appearing to 'mushroom' overnight, are like flowers in a mighty forest. Perhaps a better analogy is with handsets in a telephone system, the visible and familiar part of a massive network of cables connecting different parts of the communications 'ecosystem' lying largely unseen and unappreciated. The unseen mycelium is the real fungus, and performs invaluable work interacting with the roots of plants, and recycling matter and energy within the ecosystem.

So should you chance upon a toadstool or two as you walk by the river, stop to think about what amazing creatures we share our world with... even if their associated legends are often untrue!

PEARL-LADEN
COBWEBS

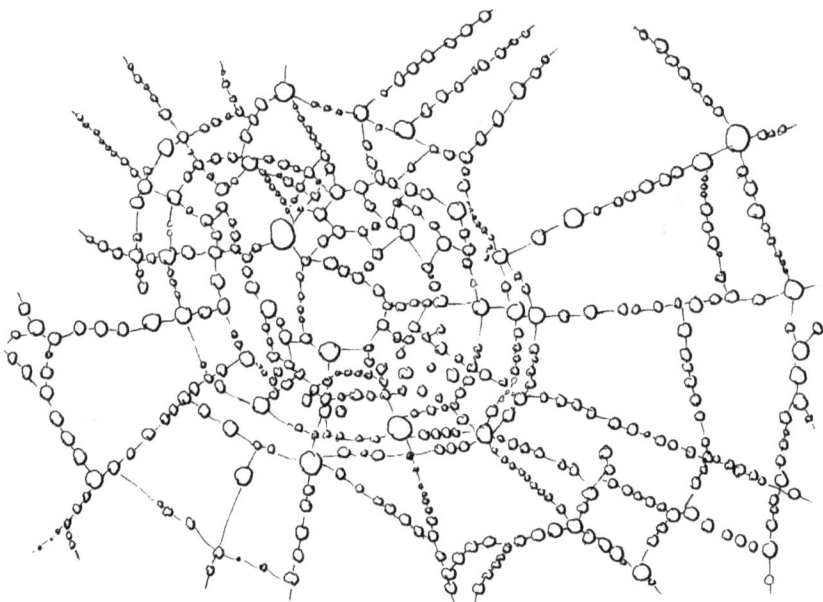

NOTHING IS QUITE as evocative of the coming of autumn as 'pearl doilies' heavy with dewdrops, liberally adorning hedgerows and tall grass on verges on still mornings.

Moisture vented into the air during shortening days condenses throughout the cooler, longer nights as a carpet of dew, jewelling grass blades, dripping from trees and captured on filigree webs spun by spider populations that have boomed on a rich diet of flying insects throughout the preceding summer.

We humans are proud of our scientific knowledge and engineering prowess. However, we are only just beginning to work out some of the mysteries of how spider silk can act so efficiently in trapping moisture from the air, capturing necklaces and networks of bright, pearl-like water drops in the morning after fogging. After all, human hair doesn't do this.

The answer lies in the microscopic structure of threads of spider silk, which recent scientific analysis has found to be an awful lot more complicated than they appear to the naked eye. Detailed microscopic observation of silk threads from the Hackled Orbweaver Spider (*Uloborus walckenaerius*), found from southern England down as far as North Africa and eastwards right to and including Japan, finds a highly complex necklace-like thread structure. What might look like simple threads to us actually comprise a core of two main fibres supporting a series of rounded 'puffs' of tiny, randomly intertwined nanofibrils. As water vapour condenses onto these puffs, they shrink into tightly packed knots, water moving towards joints between the 'puffs' where they coalesce to form larger visible droplets. This all happens due to the mystery and magic of surface tension (we considered surface tension when thinking about how Pond Skaters and other small beasties 'walk on water'), in this case reacting to the very fine structure of the spider's thread. Whether this water-capturing effect is of any evolutionary value to the spider is uncertain as webs trap insects most effectively when dry. However, evolution is rarely if ever without purpose so, who knows, maybe the droplets act as lure to attract would-be prey towards the nets or serve other functions that we are yet to suspect. These remain, like so much else in nature, mysteries yet to be explored.

Some scientists are now experimenting with artificial spider silk, using nylon fibres dipped in other plastics to mimic the microscopic structure of natural spider silk. This may potentially lead to development of new materials that enable us to collect water from 'thin air'.

Add to this the sheer strength of spider silk. The tensile strength (maximum stress a material can withstand before breaking when stretched or pulled) of spider silk is similar to steel. However, spider silk is a far less dense material meaning that, for a given weight, it is five times stronger than steel.

Even in its most everyday forms, nature is truly amazing, shaped by billions of years of evolution and with so much ingrained wisdom from which we need to learn. All the more reason to appreciate and protect the natural world, for inherent purposes but also for the many ways in which it supports our wellbeing and contains ingenious engineering, chemical and other solutions of potential utility.

All this and also inspiring us though its natural beauty, a source of much poetry and an enrichment to the spirit as nights grow longer and darker as fulsome summer recedes ever more.

And that is before we even consider spiders themselves, and their myriad roles in pest-control, as food for many birds, producing a nest lining material of choice for Wrens, and much more besides.

NOVEMBER

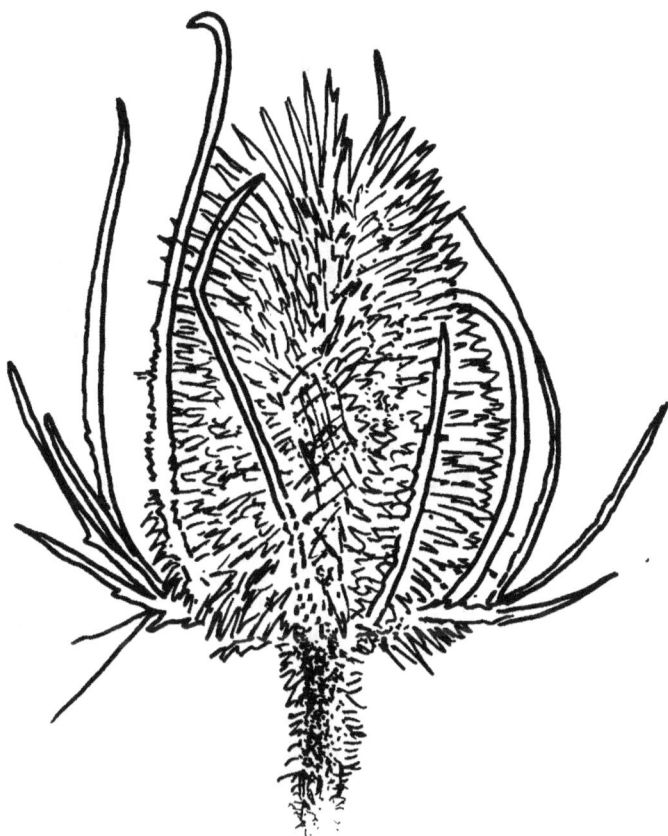

MUDDYING THE
WATER

A T THIS TIME of year, deluges of rain blow in on autumnal storms at the year's turnover. Placid rivers transform into raging torrents, whipping under bridges and scouring channels of softened vegetation and other debris. Rising floodwater predictably fans out over floodplains. Oddly, but just as predictably, people are surprised as floodwater fills valleys and inundates things unthinkingly built or grown in them.

'Flood' is hardly a cryptic component of the word 'floodplain'. Even the most cursory knowledge of geography informs us that, on average, a river will fill its floodplain every two years. That, after all, is the process by which floodplains have formed since ancient prehistory. So we should be wiser about the way we use these seasonally inundated habitats.

Pulses of water and their potential flood risks are today substantially amplified by drainage of around 90% of the wetland resources of the British Isles since Roman times. Disconnection of rivers from their floodplains and linked wetlands dramatically reduces natural flow buffering and purification processes, increasing erosive forces.

Soil loss to rivers is a major issue, and also a major cost that remains almost wholly uncounted. Firstly, there is loss of the primary resource of agriculture that may take hundreds or even thousands of years to regenerate. Secondly, substantial costs arise from the impacts of excess sediment on river ecosystems, such as clogging of gravels vital for many organisms including enabling the successful spawning of a variety of fishes, and substantial inputs of sediment-borne nutrients and other substances that perturb river ecosystems. Thirdly, we pay again through the costs of treating more contaminated water for public supply, silt removal from pipes, dams and roads, and increased dredging of navigation channels.

Soil loss accelerates massively where livestock tramples river banks, or is overstocked on steeply sloping fields or adjacent to rivers or drainage channels. It is also amplified where tillage for arable production occurs right up to the margins of rivers or ditches. These are increasingly common practices, particularly under contract farming regimes where the profit-taker has no direct financial interest in the long-term viability of farmland productivity. The craziness of modern market economics enables supermarket supply chains to take the profits of 'cheap food' without bearing the costs of its production, which we, nature and future generations instead have to bear. Many farmers, particularly on family farms, see the bigger picture and would rather act more sensitively, yet are forced instead to farm intensively for economic survival.

Across the world, soil loss is occurring at a massive scale, creating major threats for global food security. Thick brown water running off arable and livestock land is literally 'money down the drain'; a disaster in slow motion.

A range of practical, low- or no-cost and self-beneficial remedies can do much to protect vital soil resources at field and farm scale. Some examples include ploughing along contours rather than downhill, thus preventing gully erosion. Leaving 'buffer strips' of untilled or grazed vegetation between farmed areas and watercourses arrests suspended sediment, also protecting banks from scour. Relocating gates from valley bottoms to higher ground prevents sediment mobilised by intensive trampling and vehicle movements from accelerating flows of eroded soil into waterways.

Thick, brown water signals nutrients and carbon content, built up by soil-forming processes operating over centuries, going down the drain. Soil is a wealth that we must learn to love, to care for rather better, and to allow to care for us as it always has done. For personal, food security and multiple other reasons, we can no longer afford today's excessive 'muddying of the waters'.

MORE HENS!

I T WILL NOT have escaped the attention of frequent river-walkers that there are suddenly a lot more Moorhens about.

The Moorhen (*Gallinula chloropus*) – the name deriving from 'Mere Hen' and also known as the 'Water Hen' or 'Water Chicken' – is a familiar waterside bird, common across the British Isles, and I find the very same species also on wetlands I have worked on across Africa, India and the Americas.

Moorhens breed in marshy environments, well-vegetated lakes and moving waters. The first impression is that the Moorhen is black, though on closer inspection this colour is olive-brown on the back and the head and blue-grey on the underside. There is a fine, broken white line along the edge of the folded wings. Vivid white feathers are found beneath a tail generally held cocked upwards and flicked continuously as a visual warning. A striking feature of the bird is the bright red frontal shield (forehead) continuing down to the bill, which is tipped with yellow. When mature, both male and female Moorhens share this coloration and are virtually indistinguishable.

So why do we suddenly see so many more Moorhens at this time of year?

Though Moorhens have short wings, tending to escape danger by concealment rather than flight, they nevertheless can fly and some individuals do migrate. However, the biggest annual movement occurs early and late in the year across river catchments.

In spring, from late March onwards, Moorhens fan out over the countryside to form breeding territories in swamps, pools, ditches, river margins and a wide range of other water bodies. Here, they pair up and rear families, typically of a dozen 'black cotton wool' chicks. At this time, the breeding pairs become highly territorial and drive off other Moorhens, as well as any wildlife that strays too close to a floating nest made of vegetation in which both male and female birds take turns brooding the pale, speckled eggs. Moorhen pairs can raise as many as three broods in a good year.

In late autumn – now – Moorhens lose their territorial behaviour, forming gregarious groups on and adjacent to large still water bodies and rivers that are most likely to resist freezing as winter grips the landscape. So at this time, the diaspora of Moorhens scattered across damp patches in the landscape converge in numbers on suitable large water bodies.

Suddenly, more hens!

WHO DOESN'T LOVE WORMS?

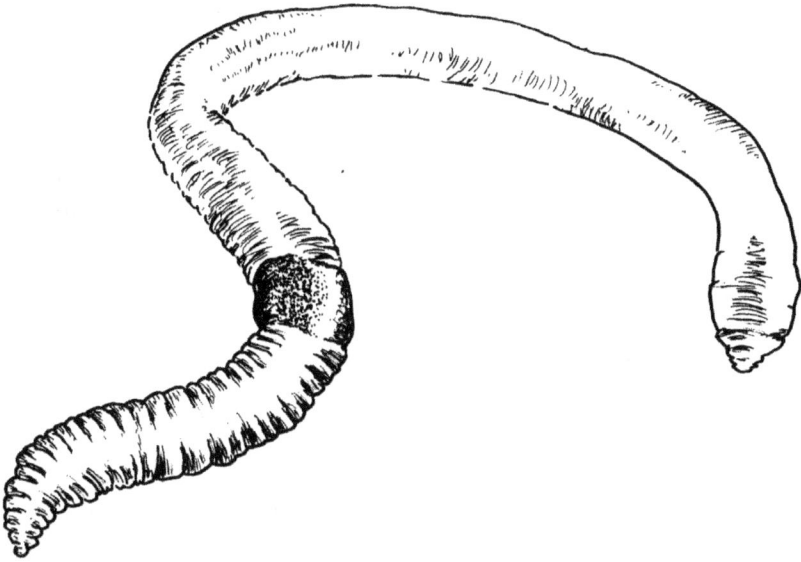

W ELL, WHO DOESN'T love worms?
    Or, perhaps I could put it better: who wouldn't love worms once
they appreciated the marvellous things they do that support our security and
wellbeing?

    Healthy soils need healthy worm populations. Worms draw down
organic matter, contributing to decomposition processes and so rebuilding
the soil's tilth and recycling nutrients benefitting the whole ecosystem.
Through their burrowing activities, worms make major, vital contributions
to oxygenation and the permeability of soils. Without worms, our soil
would be seriously degraded, less fertile and necessitating greater energy and
chemical inputs with associated financial costs to produce food and fibre
forming the basis of many economic activities let alone food security. Water
would infiltrate downwards at substantially slower rates, instead rushing off
the land surface exacerbating both erosion and downstream flood risk, also
seriously compromising replenishment of underlying groundwater and so also
contributing to water shortages and drought risk.

Earthworms are also known as the 'Blackbird's favourite', providing important food for many species of bird from blackbirds and thrushes to buzzards and kites. Badgers forage for worms, particularly in winter when other food is scarce, as do foxes, shrews and voles. Worms also are the mainstay of moles, which seek them out in moist soils. And, as many anglers know, a huge diversity of fish species – from the smallest stickleback to the mightiest salmon – can't resist a juicy worm.

The importance of worms to farming, the water cycle and wider biodiversity can't be over-estimated.

There are 25 species of earthworm in Britain, and around 6,000 known species worldwide. (Without getting into too much biological complexity, I'm just talking of the annelids, or segmented worms here, and not flatworms, nematodes, flukes and other elongated beasties generally tagged as 'worms'.) Some earthworms are aquatic, but many live in terrestrial soils preferring some moisture including in floodplains but also on higher grounds where they burrow downwards to follow the water in dry conditions.

Britain's largest earthworm is the Lobworm (*Lumbricus terrestris*), or 'Common Earthworm', up to 12 centimetres (nearly five inches) long and living in vertical burrows up to 3 metres (nine feet) deep from which they emerge at night to feed on fallen leaves and other decaying plant material and to mate with adjacent worms. Our many smaller worm species include the often red-and-yellow striped Brandling worm (*Eisenia fetida*) found commonly in compost and other moist decaying leaf litter, organic-rich soils and manure heaps. Also, the hardy, banded reddish-brown Dendrobaena (or 'European Nightcrawler', *Eisenia hortensis*) that is usually found in woodland litter and soils rich in organic matter, a worm popular as an angling bait but also increasingly used in composting. There are many more British worm species, and even an Earthworm Society of Britain that aims to promote and support scientific research about earthworms, their environments and their conservation.

A persistent myth, still often repeated, is that if you cut a worm in two then each half will regenerate into a new worm. In reality, cutting a worm in half results simply in a dead worm! Though apparently simple, worms are in fact complex organisms with a mouth at the front, a long gut to extract organic matter from ingested soil and decaying vegetation, an anus at the rear, and associated vascular, reproductive and other organs *en route*.

The Ancient Greek philosopher Aristotle (384-322 BC) called earthworms the "*Earth's guts*" as they act like intestines by processing the soil's organic matter and turning it into food for plants. The Egyptian Queen Cleopatra (69-30 BC) recognised the contribution of earthworms to Egyptian agriculture, declaring them to be sacred by law.

So, who now doesn't love worms?

THE RIPARIAN
PHARMACOPOEIA

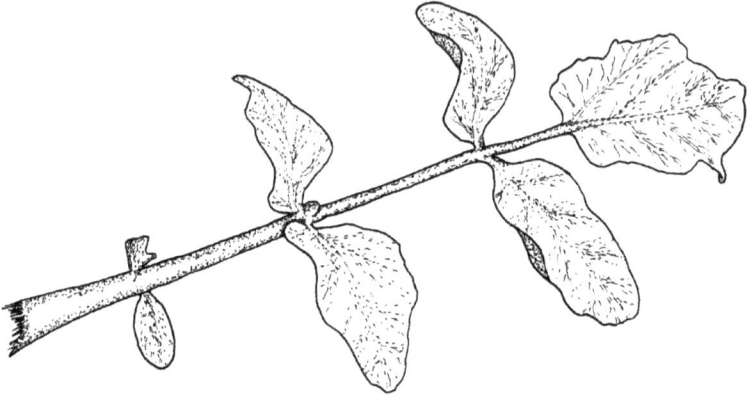

OFTEN, I WORK in the Himalayas on rivers and forests, as well as in desert regions of India, where people live in close interdependence with living things and natural processes. One fascinating aspect of this symbiosis is Ayurvedic medicine, encapsulating centuries of localised knowledge about the properties of plants.

One of my studies on the wetlands of the desert edge of Rajasthan found virtually every plant species had Ayurvedic uses, whilst most animals – particularly birds and fish – had profound spiritual and cultural significance.

We shouldn't be surprised about the biologically active properties of plants. Extracts of tea and coffee are everyday examples. If you are rooted in one spot, how do you defend yourself against species that would graze or infect you, and how do you communicate? Plants have engaged in billions of years of chemical warfare, innovating compounds serving myriad purposes.

Traditional uses of riverbank willow as a pain-killer led to synthesis of aspirin, managing pain, fever and inflammation; the willow genus *Salix* gives its name to salicylic acid from which aspirin (acetylsalicylic acid) is derived.

Hemlock (*Conium maculatum*) is common on our riverbanks, famed for its use in poisoning Greek philosopher Socrates when condemned to death for impiety and corrupting the young men of Athens in 399 BC. It was also an ingredient used by witches in Shakespeare's Macbeth. Current medicinal applications of Hemlock including treatment of breathing problems, suppression of pain and management of anxiety, mania, spasms, skin infections, epilepsy, Parkinson's disease, bladder infections and reversal of strychnine poisoning.

Deadlier still is the more common waterside Hemlock Water-dropwort (*Oenanthe crocata*), every part of which is potentially fatal containing the powerful convulsant *oenanthotoxin*. No British wild plant is responsible for more fatal accidents, generally when mistaken for Coriander (leaves) or Parsnip (tubers). The plant was deployed to poison rats and moles. Though not an approved medicine, small doses have been deployed to treat eruptive skin diseases in humans and cattle.

The springtime Celandine (*Ficaria verna*) is also known as Pilewort as its bulbous tubers resemble the human condition that the plant was used to treat. Extracts of Tansy (*Tanacetum vulgare*) were produced to treat intestinal worms, rheumatism, digestive problems, fevers and sores, and to induce abortions as well as, counterintuitively, help women conceive. Despite most medicinal applications being discredited, Tansy nevertheless remains a component of some medicines and is listed by the United States Pharmacopoeia as a treatment for fevers, feverish colds and jaundice.

Add to this many proven beneficial uses of Stinging Nettles (*Urtica dioica*) including for urinary issues, osteoarthritis and joint pain, hay fever, bleeding and eczema, not to mention as a source of fibre from which clothes can be made. The leaves of Comfrey (*Symphytum officinale*) are a principal ingredient in healing salves treating wounds, scratches, sunburn and other skin irritations, and as a tea to treat coughs, congestion and asthma. Other common riverside plants such as Meadowsweet, Red Campion, various species of willowherb, Woody Nightshade, Arrowhead, Watercress, Angelica, Alder, Elder and Ash and many more possess multiple medicinal properties.

In the 'global north', we may look down upon the masses in the developing world who cannot afford to access the miracles of modern medicine. But the reality is that traditional practices encode deep indigenous knowledge. Also, let us not forget that many chemical compounds and most chemical families developed into manufactured pharmaceuticals derive from natural sources, discovered and commercialised by the now £ multi-billion bioprospecting industry.

Have we allowed the accumulated wealth of centuries of traditional knowledge – knowledge we may need in future – to slip away beneath our feet, even as we walk through the riparian pharmacopoeia?

THE SEASON OF THE PLOVER

I RECALL CLOUDS of Plovers working the damp winter fields of my youth, taking to the wing in their droves. Their far-off call – 'pee-wit' – evoked winter, and accounted for one of their various common names 'Peewit'. Their wavering flight on lapping, broad wings, black above and white below, was a kind of visual onomatopoeia of another common name: 'Lapwing'. The bird is also known as the 'Northern Plover', and also the 'Green Plover' on the basis of the iridescence of its superficially black and white plumage.

I speak here of the Common Plover (*Vanellus vanellus*), a formerly familiar farmland bird that has regrettably suffered significant declines particularly since the 1970s due in substantial measure to widespread land drainage and changes in farming practices. Indeed, so perilous has their decline been that they are now classified as 'Near Threatened' on the IUCN (International Union for the Conservation of Nature) 'Red List' of globally endangered species.

The Common Plover is just one of many birds known as Plovers in the British Isles, all members of the Plover and lapwing family (*Charadriidae*) and including the Dotterel, Golden Plover, Grey Plover, Little-ringed Plover and the Ringed Plover. None are faring well, as all are waders dependent on the increasingly scarce habitat of wet meadows and other forms of wetland with short vegetation.

Though the Great Bustard is the county bird of Wiltshire, it is the Common Plover that is on the logo of the Wiltshire Wildlife Trust as one of the county's most characteristic birds. Regrettably, the declining trend of Plovers in Wiltshire is as grave as, or graver than, anywhere else.

Whilst Lapwings are with us all year round, they tend to move around to find habitat suited to their varying seasonal needs. Typically, they are birds of farmland, particularly in lowland areas. In the spring breeding season they prefer habitat such as spring sown cereals, root crops, permanent unimproved pasture, meadows and fallow fields, and can also be found on wetlands with short vegetation often moving to higher ground. As the chicks hatch from ground-level nests, they need to have access to wet grassland to feed. In increasingly uniform landscapes, the juxtaposition of suitable dry and wet habitats in this critical life phase is in short supply. During winter, Lapwings tend to gather in large flocks, the native population bolstered by birds in passage on their migrations around their wide Eurasian distribution. Common Plovers overwinter on suitable extensive areas of pasture and ploughed fields, also making use of estuaries and other broad muddy wet habitats though needing to retreat to nearby undisturbed grassland at high tide. Common Lapwings feed on a variety of worms, insects and small crustaceans that they extract from wet soil, a food source often limited by increasing farming intensity and agrochemicals.

Scottish mythology has it that Plovers have the souls of young mothers who die in childbirth. In Greek mythology, Agron so displeased the three Gods, Hermes, Athena and Artemis, that Hermes changed him into a Plover. Plovers' eggs were an expensive delicacy in Victorian Britain, mentioned in Evelyn Waugh's *Brideshead Revisited*. In the Netherlands, there remains a traditional competition to find the first Peewit egg of the year (*het eerste kievietsei*), the province Friesland at one time granted an exception for cultural-historical reasons against the European Union-wide prohibition on gathering their eggs.

I miss the sight of flocks of these charismatic birds, once so common over winter floodplains but now with sporadic small flocks a rare and notable sighting bringing warmth to a cold winter day by the water.

DECEMBER

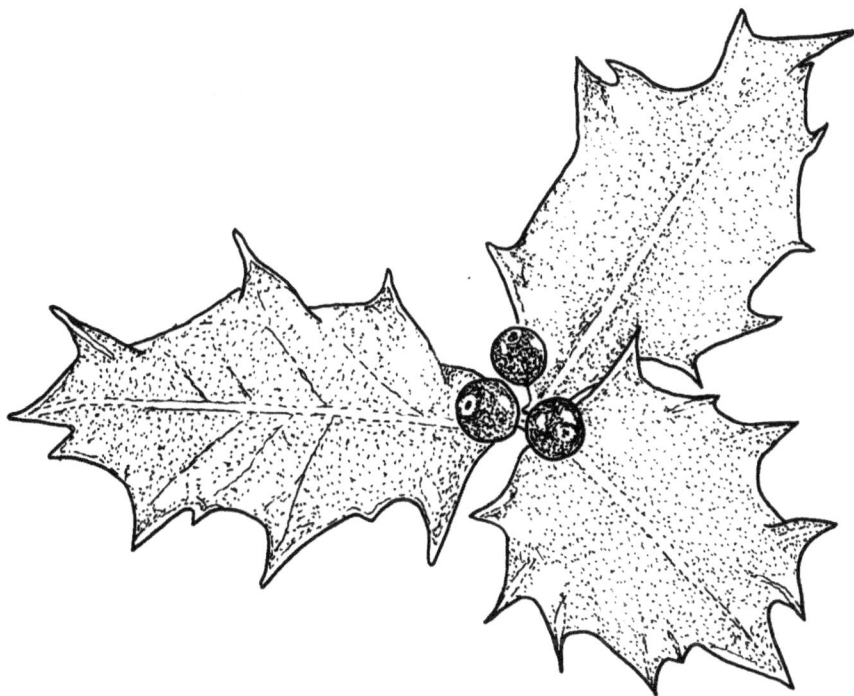

RED-BREASTED
COMPANIONS

A NYONE REGULARLY SPENDING quiet time by the river or in the garden
may attract a feathered friend.

Robins are as familiar as Christmas, as gaudy though distinctively
clad year-round. Their fluting whistle brightens the day nearly all year, and
sometimes at night near street lights. Robins don't migrate, remaining with
us throughout the most inhospitable weather when food and cheer are limited.
It's unsurprising to learn that *Erithacus rubecula* was adopted as the UK's
unofficial national bird in the 1960s, consistently featuring in polls as Britain's
favourite bird.

Robins seemingly enjoy proximity to people. Anglers, always with
bait to hand, are the Robin's waterside friends. On well-fished waters,
particularly in winter, one of these cheeky birds is often seen hopping around
nearby, or perching on a fishing rod or close branch eying up the angler to
charm them out of a maggot or worm, even taking it from the hand. Though
'The angler's companion', Robins are also 'The gardener's friend' following
gardeners around closely, perching on a fork handle in anticipation, and
commonly nesting in watering cans or similar shelter in the potting shed.

But anglers and gardeners don't enjoy undivided loyalty from these red-breasted charmers. Though many wild birds fare poorly through urban sprawl and agricultural intensification, Robins do well in woodland, hedgerows, scrub by riverbanks and lakes, parks, urban gardens and outbuildings, courting attention on urban balconies, patios or around the barbeque. The UK is home to nearly six million Robin breeding territories. Throughout history Robins have been noted as the friends of urbanites, the Norse, storytellers, saviours, those in Purgatory, songwriters and sportsmen.

Though flattering, warming a chilly day by the river, this 'friendship' comprises a major dose of cat-like 'cupboard love'. Robins don't just 'buddy up' with humans, but form bonds with wild animals like boar, deer and others that disturb the ground exposing beak-sized morsels. Robins 'love' us as we turn the earth, carry tubs of fishing bait or, like sentimental fools, throw them tit-bits if they incline their heads in a coquettish way!

Found throughout Europe, eastwards to Siberia and southwards to Algeria and some Atlantic islands, Robins have been hunted along with other small birds in some countries. However, many nations and the British in particular love them! We put their images on cards and stamps, tell stories and make up songs. Norse mythology held the Robin as a storm-cloud bird sacred to Thor, God of Thunder. One British folk tale explains the Robin's distinctive breast, originally brown, as a mark from the blood of Jesus on the cross as the Robin flew down to his side, singing into his ear to comfort him. Another legend tells that the bird's breast was scorched fetching water for souls in Purgatory. Robins also feature in children's tales, such as the macabre *Babes in the Wood* covering the children's dead bodies. The association between Robins and Christmas is less ancient than generally assumed, thought to arise from postmen in Victorian Britain who wore red uniforms and were nicknamed 'Robin'.

The Robin's charm and mellifluous song, however, belies a murderous reality. Robins sing as they are fiercely territorial, defending a fiefdom all year round against all comers with often lethal force. Males and females only share a territory during the spring and summer breeding season, raising up to three broods of 5-7 eggs. Many Robins without territories die well before their first year, more so during severe winters. That ubiquitous song is in reality little more than a death threat to would-be intruders, including defending access to their human 'friends'!

DECEMBER MOTHS

WHEN WALKING THE river banks into dusk or night time in the depths of winter, you may be surprised by the ghostly flutter of a pale moth. Perhaps you dismiss it as a play of dappled moonlight. But you will have seen these intrepid insects undeniably from time to time when driving at night. Why on earth would a moth fly around when temperatures are crashing below zero and no nectar-bearing flowers are available as food?

There is a species of moth known as the December Moth (*Poecilocampa populi*) that is both widespread and common throughout much of Britain, taking to the wing at night any time between October and early January. This is a reasonably large moth, male insects with a wingspan of around 2½ inches (about 6.5 centimetres), a handsome insect with pale grey to brown forewings crossed with a narrow, wavy cream-white stripe. Females, a half-inch or so bigger, have a more translucent appearance due to a lower density of fine scales covering their wings.

But why fly in the depths of winter when no food is available? As we constantly discover, nature is full of surprising and innovative survival strategies. Bats, a principal predator of adult moths, are almost absent in mid-winter, so the moths can fly with little threat from these small mammals as indeed from many insectivorous birds that have either migrated away or which need good light to feed.

So what do the adult moths feed on? Nothing! As adults, December moths are unable to feed, lacking the necessary mouth parts. Instead, stored energy keeps the adult moths active in pursuit of mates. After mating, eggs are laid on food plants where they remain dormant until the spring. Whilst many moth and butterfly species depend on a highly specific food plant, the food plants of December Moths are surprisingly catholic and include a wide range of broadleaved tree species including Oaks, Birches, Elms, Hawthorns, Blackthorn, Sallow and various species of poplar. December Moth caterpillars can be found on these trees from April to June, feeding on their leaves by night and resting up on twigs or bark throughout the day. Once fully developed, the caterpillars pupate under the bark, or else amongst plant debris, emerging as adult moths once winter approaches.

Owing to their affinity with these woody species, December Moths are mainly found in woodland but also amongst scrub, hedgerows and well-established gardens. Hence, one can encounter them not uncommonly in shrubby or wooded ground near the river or along country lanes.

December Moths are far from the only species of winter-flying moth found across Britain. Another such is the extravagantly-named Feathered Thorn (*Colotois pennaria*), so named for its exquisitely feathered antennae, flying from August to December.

The females of some winter-flying moth species, such as the Mottled Umber (*Erannis defoliaria*) and the Winter Moth (*Operophtera brumata*) seen on the wing from November to February, are flightless. The wings of female moths are no more than tiny vestigial features, another of nature's clever survival strategies enabling females to divert their energies into egg production rather than flight. Male moths are attracted to females by pheromones: hormones released from their flightless bodies and carried on night breezes.

So how do moth species with flightless females disperse, given the highly restricted distance female moths can crawl between emergence and egg-laying? Many do so as caterpillars, using a technique known as 'ballooning' in which small caterpillars crawl up to a high point then produce a long strand of silk that, like a spinnaker, gets caught in the breeze carrying the tiny grub aloft for sometimes prodigious distances.

Nature, as ever, is wonderful and constantly surprising, ever elegant in its adaptation of form and lifestyle to the functions of survival and perpetuation.

WHERE THE WILD THINGS ARE

A S I WRITE, the river is responding to recent rains with its first significant flush of autumn. Although our increasingly unstable climate makes timing less predictable, we can expect more rainfall on the journey through to winter and with it a rise in the river's pace, height and turbidity. Most years, we can expect the river to fan out over the floodplain; that, after all, is why they are called FLOODplains, how they were formed, and why building on them remains a stupid idea.

When the river rises to a swirling maelstrom, affording us a lesson in humility as it sweeps whole branches and trees and all manner of flotsam in its wake, do you ever stop to wonder how on earth all that tiny river life survives such seeming brutality? Hatchlings from this year's fish spawn, for example, will be barely as long as the width of your little finger and the invertebrates upon which they feed are even smaller.

River creatures endure floods in four principal ways.

Firstly, a walk on the floodplain during a rising spate will reveal small fish following the relatively calm fingers of water creeping out through the coarse grass. You can see the Kingfisher hunting these food-rich margins too and, although fish have an eerie instinct to follow the falling flood back, some inevitably get stranded in dips in the floodplain and here Grey Herons too may join the feast.

Secondly, beneath the maelstrom and foam of the river's surface, far more placid flows and back eddies are to be found deeper down as friction against irregularities on the river bed and margins creates the phenomenon of laminar flow. Here, fish both big and small as well as invertebrates can ride out the rush of water passing overhead.

Thirdly, mobile river life retreats beneath and within rocks and vegetation, both living and dead, or buries itself in the sediment as a place of refuge. This is why habitat is vital at these times, and we can help the river with wise management, retaining diverse habitat and compensating for historic habitat loss, reinforcing ecosystem resilience.

Finally, some creatures evade floods entirely, be that by seeking out quiet side-channels and connected wetlands or hunkering down into deep holes and perennial weed beds. Others have resting life stages such as eggs or pupae that are less vulnerable to surging flows.

I am always delighted by the seasonal miracle of late winter and early spring when, with the first sense of returning light and clearer, calmer water, the river margins suddenly blossom anew with Minnows and fry of other fish species, and caddis larvae can be seen dragging their cases along the river bed.

Nature – its beauty but also its tenacity in the face of extremes – is a perennial source of wonder and inspiration, deserving our attention and respect.

MOBILE HOMES IN
THE SILT

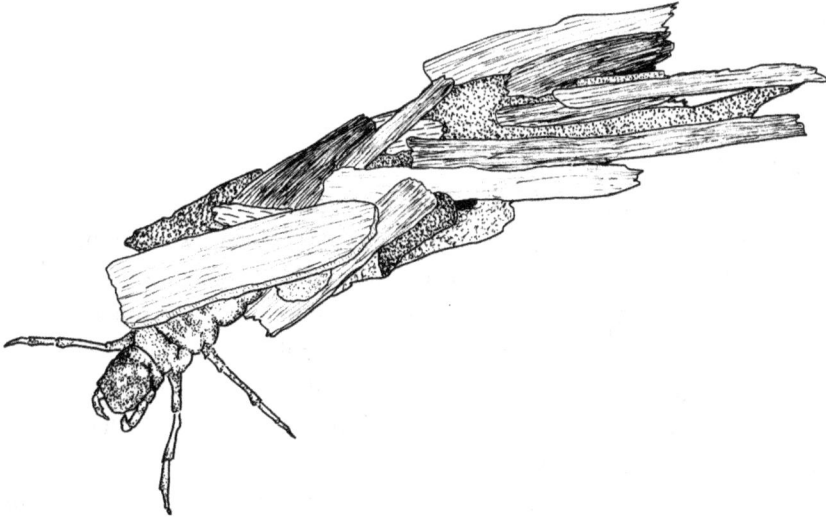

ONE OF MANY aquatic creatures that have entranced me since childhood
is the caddis larva. Peer into the river's margin as the water clarifies in
late winter, spring and summer and you may see little bundles of twigs, leaves
or small stones an inch or two long that, on closer scrutiny, are moving slowly
and jerkily. Most likely, these are larvae of a wide variety of species of caddis
flies. Quite literally, caddis larvae build 'mobile homes' of various substances
around their elongated bodies, connected with sticky silk, for camouflage and
protection. Case material can be species-specific, as can habitat from small
pools to powerful rivers.

Caddis flies have a four-stage life cycle. Larvae hatch from eggs laid on
or in the water, growing through a series of moults over one or two years.
Caddis species with cased larvae are general herbivores, shredding leaves and
other large organic matter or scraping algae from submerged surfaces. But not
all caddis build cases. Some lack cases and subsist as mobile predators on other
insects or small invertebrates, often attached by a silk thread to avoid being
washed away. Other caddis larvae spin silk nets to catch free-floating plant or
small animal matter from passing water, one family also building fixed cases
firmly attached to plants or other submerged surfaces.

Fully developed larvae metamorphose into silk-wrapped pupae attached to hard underwater surfaces. Adult caddis flies eventually emerge to climb or float to the surface, taking to the air generally towards the end of the day in spring or summer. Sometimes they do so in dense clouds. Some can also be nocturnal. Caddis flies superficially resemble small moths, to which they are closely related, but can be identified by their long, veined wings folded backwards tent-like over the abdomen at rest, their long, forward-pointing antennae, and the covering of fine hairs over most of their bodies and wings. (This feature gives the order *Trichoptera* its Latin name from the Greek words: 'trichos' = hair; 'ptera' = wing.)

To fly fishermen, caddis are known as sedge flies owing to their habit of climbing up emergent vegetation, such as sedges, when taking to the air. Many patterns of artificial fly imitate different caddis species, the commonest and in my experience most useful being the 'Grannom Fly'. (Grannom typically emerge in late spring.) Trout, Chub, Grayling, Dace and many other fish species eagerly take caddis flies, and also swallow larvae whole, case and all, as they are a large and nutrient-rich food source of particular value to spring-spawning fish species.

Like many insects with aquatic life stages, the adult is shorter-lived than the larva. Lifespans of different species vary, but can be up to a month. Adult flies feed on nectar with their simple mouthparts, but their main function is to breed and disperse eggs, generally migrating upstream to compensate for the effect of downstream drift on larvae. A female caddis may lay up to 800 eggs. Some release eggs on the surface, leaving them to sink with no further care. Others pull themselves underwater, often using vegetation and with a film of air trapped by the fine hairs giving them a silvery appearance, to deposit eggs on the river bed before floating back to the surface.

My fascination though is more than just biological and piscatorial. The intricate cases of caddis are things of beauty, and their wonderful adaptation of constructing and inhabiting 'mobile homes' for much of their lives is truly fascinating to watch and wonder. Do spend some time as the water clears to enjoy these little marvels of nature.

FLYING KITTENS

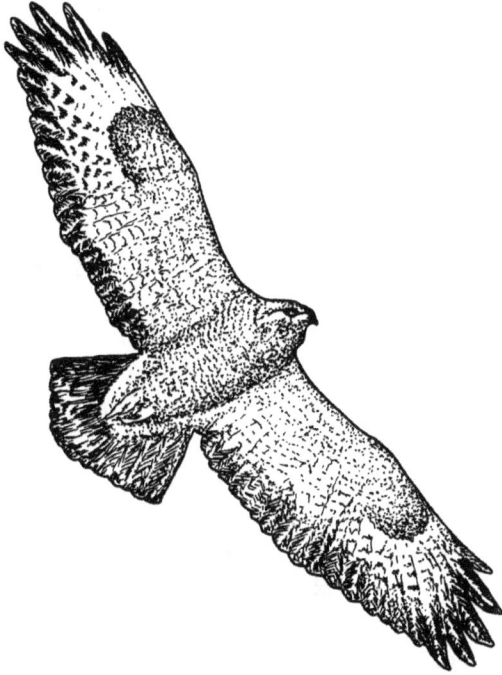

A N EVOCATIVE SOUND heard across our landscapes throughout the year, frequently prominent in the winter, is the mew of flying kittens. It is often best appreciated in lowland river valleys.

Flying kittens? If you walk our rivers, you will, I am sure, have heard a plaintiff mewing particularly on bright and stiller days. You may look into the vegetation for what sounds like a kitten, or perhaps some other smaller mammal. You may scan hedgerows or woodlands for the hiding culprit. But look upwards and you will in all probability spot the source of the cries.

There you will as often as not observe one or more Buzzards (*Buteo buteo*) soaring on broad, rounded wings, scanning the terrain and calling to mates, progeny and others of their species.

The plaintive mew of a Buzzard on the wing is often mistaken for a cat. But the Buzzard is a large predatory bird. Its characteristically broad and rounded wings can be greater than 130 cm (54 inches) in span with a body mass of potentially 1.3 kg (3lb). The neck and tail are short. In global terms this is a medium-sized raptor (bird of prey), but it is a large bird by British standards (albeit only a tenth of the weight or our heaviest bird, the Mute Swan: *Cygnus olor*).

Buzzards are now the commonest and most widespread bird of prey in the British Isles. When soaring or gliding, the broad wings seldom flap but instead are held in a shallow 'V' to ride thermal currents as the bird scans the landscape below for food.

The Buzzard is a resident or, at best, short migrant species. Though small flocks may be migrating birds, they are far more commonly a group of parent and progeny flying together as the younger and parent birds tend to remain together during the winter period. I have seen as many as ten over our house at one time, most probably two families co-mingling, as Buzzards can be common where habitat is good.

Breeding in the summer, Buzzards need trees for nesting. However, they tend to hunt over more open land where they feed on small mammals, birds and carrion, resorting to earthworms and large insects when other prey is limited.

A familiar sight today, these 'flying kittens' were scarce some thirty years ago. The reasons for this are varied, but a key factor was bioaccumulation of pesticides. Bioaccumulation – build-up of persistent substances in prey animals that then get passed as a progressively larger dose up food chains with top-level predators accumulating disproportionately high body loads – was responsible for the former demise of the Otter, Sparrowhawk, Kestrel and other of our predators. Despite the plethora of serious environmental issues we still face, progressive phase-out of the worst types of persistent pesticides put into widespread use since the post-Second World War era has enabled the natural recovery and spread of these once declining charismatic species: a real success story since the nadir and grave prognosis of then current trends described in Rachel Carson's evocative 1962 book *Silent Spring*.

Buzzards are a protected and still recovering species, though limited licences are granted under strict conditions to control numbers affecting pheasants reared for the shooting industry. They are certainly a bird that deserves our respect as a charismatic element of our natural wealth, an indicator of success in tackling a pernicious environmental problem, and as part of the natural heritage and soundscape of our winter river valleys.

Next time you're walking the river, listen out and look up for the uplifting presence of these 'flying kittens'.

JANUARY

CRUSTY CREATURES

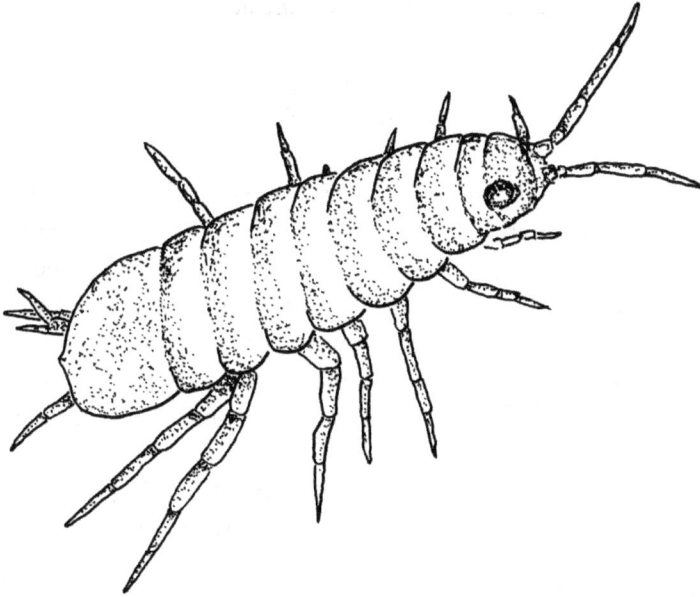

M UCH OF RIVER life becomes torpid during the winter. Some, such as
fishes and particularly younger life stages, seek out gentler flows and
more tangled habitat in which they can expend less energy fighting stronger
currents and subsist on reduced availability of food. Others such as many
insects enter resting phases in their life cycles, or else like Pond Skaters go into
hibernation or near-hibernating stasis. Bats above the water's surface go into full
hibernation in sheltered, dry places, whilst birds such as Swallows, Swifts and
Sand and House Martins and many warbler species migrate to warmer climes.

However, some creatures remain present and active all year round. Water
snails are one such group as too, though more cryptic in the sediment yet very
common and widespread, are various species of freshwater mussels from tiny Pea
Mussels (*Pisidium* species) to the large Swan Mussel (*Anodonta cygnea*).

More conspicuous, at least if you turn over stones or disturb leaf litter,
are a range of crustaceans. Amongst the under-stone dwelling crustaceans
most commonly encountered in our rivers are crayfish and shrimps, whilst
Water Slaters are more common in poorer water quality or hiding in decaying
vegetation in river edges.

The native White-clawed Crayfish (*Austropotamobius pallipes*) is, as described previously, now largely extirpated in many parts of Britain by the spread of more aggressive, plague-carrying alien species, particularly the American Signal Crayfish (*Pacifastacus leniusculus*).

The most common of the freshwater shrimp species found in our rivers is *Gammarus pulex*, the 'pulex' name denoting its flea-like ability to jump when stranded on damp land. This and several other species also occur in ponds, particularly those with inflowing streams and springs.

A recent species that has invaded British rivers from its native Ponto-Caspian region of eastern Europe is the 'Killer Shrimp' (*Dikerogammarus villosus*), the shrimp progressively advancing across western Europe and appearing in British waters in 2010 and spreading subsequently now quite widely. Killer Shrimps can colonise many types of habitat, tolerating a range of temperatures as well as oxygen concentrations and even mild salinity, living a predatory lifestyle feeding on a variety of invertebrates and breeding all year round.

More gentle in habit and also native are the Water Slaters, looking similar to woodlice to which they are a close aquatic relative. For those who wish to look more closely, the Common Water Slater (*Asellus aquaticus*) can be distinguished by the two white spots on its head whereas the less common One-spotted Water Slater (*Asellus meridianus*) has, unsurprisingly given its name, only one spot. The Common Water Slater is by far the more common of the two, found in a wide diversity of ponds and river margins. As Water Slaters can exist in water with a low oxygen content and subsist by eating rotting vegetation, performing the important services of recycling stored nutrients and energy into the food chain, they tend to fare well in richer and more polluted waters which are also less favourable to their potential predators.

Even these apparently boring creatures are truly fascinating, Water Slaters moulting periodically as do all crustaceans. Shedding the exoskeleton (external skeleton) enables them to grow and, in so doing, enabling them to completely regenerate lost limbs and recover from other major injuries. But Water Slaters are also marsupials, the female slater laying eggs during warmer months into her brood pouch, or marsupium, comprising overlapping, flat blades extending from the anterior legs enabling the mother to hold and protect her developing brood under her body until the larvae are sufficiently developed to emerge as miniature versions of the adults.

As the crusty exoskeleton giving the crustaceans their name contains a significant amount of calcium carbonate (which we most commonly experience as chalk or limestone), the crustaceans fare best in hard water and are consequently scarcer in acid waters and so generally absent from more mountainous uplands or acid heathland.

BOTH SIDES NOW

W E BRITISH HAVE a well-known obsession with the weather, which constitutes a constant feature, or at least punctuation, of many conversations. But then, we do have rather a lot of it.

I recall a hazy April day in rural Rajasthan (India's northern desert state), asking the village headman if rain was on the way. After a moment's reflection, gazing skywards, he shook his head and said, " *No, not until September*". (September is the end of the monsoon period; the monsoon did not occur at all that year, creating real hardships, so he was sort of right.) Many parts of Southern Europe, mid-continental USA and regions of the tropics live with such seasonal certainties. Furniture is moved outside where it will not be spoiled by dew and rain until the weather breaks, with any splashes from sporadic showers drying quickly in the low humidity with little harm.

Our small islands just happen to be situated where south-westerly prevailing winds, carrying warmth and moisture from the Gulf Stream, butt up against the polar air space. Condensation leads to formation of many clouds, high rainfall and background humidity. As the jet stream – a fast-moving ribbon of air flow running west-to-east some 9 to 16 kilometres above the Earth's surface – kicks south, cool polar conditions prevail. As it kicks north, we enjoy the warmer, moist wash of Atlantic flows.

Where these two air cells meet, clouds are a given. We are, in geographic terms, blessed by a high frequency of overcast skies and a mixture of forms of precipitation from rain to sleet, snow, hail and drizzle. The weather we get on any particular day and place is the luck of the draw, dictated by the current status of this eternal aerial tussle.

Perhaps we don't appreciate then what a great place the British Isles is to watch clouds. We have so many and such a wide diversity of them. At high altitude, we enjoy the delicate filaments of cirrus, fibrous veils of cirrostratus, and patchy sheets of cirrocumulus. At mid altitudes, we have sheet-like altostratus, laminated rolls of altocumulus, and the thick, rain-bearing continuum of nimbostratus. Then, at lower elevation, we see the familiar, cauliflower-like mounds of cumulus, uniform layers of stratus, towering cumulonimbus with rising anvil heads generating hail, tornadoes and heavy rain, and the honeycombed layer of stratocumulus. As with many of nature's gifts, perhaps we Brits take our rich cloudscape too much for granted?

Consequently, the British Isles are generally well-watered, though the pattern of precipitation is far from uniform. Geographical location combines with the heterogeneity of geology and topography to generate mixed weather. As moist, oceanic air flows hit land and are deflected upwards, cooling condenses water into droplets. This is why, for example, we often see fog rolling in on the coast or hanging over hills. Meanwhile, England's south-east is in a 'rain shadow', where prevailing west and south-westerly air flows have already dropped their moisture and rainfall is lowest exactly where the human population is at its greatest density, with rainfall per capita famously lower than in Libya. This situation creates a wealth and wide diversity of rivers, pools, lakes, bogs, fens and other wetlands across our home islands, as well as human pressures upon them.

So, on a cloudy day, or when the rain washes out our plans, perhaps we should reflect on our global geographical context and relative freedom from water poverty. The British cloudscape and propensity to dampness is, in reality, something special to be treasured rather than about which to complain!

THE 'JENNY WREN'

THE RIVER BANK is perhaps at its most barren in the month of January. Scoured by flood, rain and wind, ravaged by white frosts, the banksides of the river lay bare, bright Celandines yet to open their sulphurous faces to the lengthening day. Silt and nettle roots intersperse sporadic riparian trees, their gnarled fingers dipping to trap a strand-line of bleached straw from last year's willow-herb species and Cleavers. A Roe Deer may elegantly pace the bank top, seeking green shoots and bark, wide-eyed with pricked ears, ever-vigilant on willowy legs, its breath misting the cold, still air under clear blue skies.

After menacing skies bringing sleet and storm, the arrival of an anticyclone may waft in as a blessed relief as high atmospheric pressure pushes away the glowering cover of clouds. The cost, however, is sharp frosts and biting cold by night, though these are benignly twinned by calm, crisp days under cool blue skies.

Far from cowed by climatic adversity, life that had neither withdrawn to over-winter underground, in burrows, under stones, in leaf mounds nor to foreign lands now positively bustles in the denuded river valley.

A loud, proud and mellifluous voice calls out from the base of a sallow tree, leaning precariously over the chill waters. It is amazing that such a tiny

scrap of feather and flesh, one of Britain's smallest birds, can sound so gigantic!
Hyperactive amongst the dried herbage and the frost-bare trunks of riverside
trees, a tiny Wren hops and flits in its incessant hunt for dormant insect life,
all the while singing the joy of life to all that would listen or would encroach
upon its territory.

This troglodyte – the Wren has the Latin name of *Troglodytes
troglodytes* literally means 'cave-dweller' after its habit of hunting out insect
food in recesses – may not be the smallest British bird. That honour falls
jointly to the Firecrest (*Regulus ignicapilla*) and the Goldcrest (*Regulus
regulus*) each with a body length of only 9 centimetres, but the Eurasian Wren
is not far behind them at 9-10 centimetres. Found throughout Europe and
eastwards through Asia from northern Iran and Afghanistan across to Japan,
the Wren is most generally resident throughout the year and only migratory in
the extreme north of its range.

The fortunes of the 'Jenny Wren' at human hand has not always been
benign, particularly around the turn of the year. Indeed, humans have
treated them dreadfully for much of the past few hundred years. These poor
and harmless birds had been hunted or otherwise persecuted widely across
Europe in medieval times. In parts of Ireland and some other places across
the continent, this practice continues in the present day. This is down to
two superstitions that cast damning aspersions upon what is one of our most
charming, familiar and harmless native birds.

The first superstition relates to the supposed arrogance of the humble
Wren. Fable had it that all the birds one day determined to see which could fly
the highest in the air to determine who was truly the king. Slowly, each fell
by the wayside, leaving only the mighty eagle high in the sky. When the eagle
had flown as high as it could go, it proudly proclaimed itself the king of all
the birds. Then, suddenly, a little Wren that had hidden amongst the eagle's
feathers emerged to fly upwards, 'higher than an eagle', boasting that it was
the true king!

The second superstition demonises the poor bird for alleged betrayal of
Saint Stephen, the first Christian martyr imprisoned by Jewish authorities for
his beliefs. He was reputedly on the point of escape from sleeping warders
until a Wren sang and roused the guards; poor Stephen was subsequently
stoned to death. Consequently, every Boxing Day (Saint Stephen's day),
Wrens were killed and carried round in a holly bush. The ceremony is little
practised today although, for all its innocence, many a Wren is still slaughtered

and displayed by the 'Wren Boys Procession' in some parts of Ireland where superstition and prejudice persist against this harmless, amiable bird. The traditional 'Feeding the Wren' ceremony, most often performed by young people to ask for money, is often accompanied by the chant: "*The Wren, the Wren, the king of all birds. On Saint Stephen's day was caught in the furze*".

Fortunately, on its otherwise barren bank, Wrens sing loud and bold by the lazy winter river, whilst much other river life lies torpid from the biting chill of sleet, storm and frosts that paint the grass and tree tops in a shroud of air frost.

The day and the season is brighter for the Wren, to which I always offer a few words of gratitude that turn to steam in the chill mid-winter air.

SEASONS GONE WILD

A S MANY PEOPLE are remarking, nature is doing weird things.
There were certainly plenty of floristic anomalies around the river and
my home village in Wiltshire during the first week of January 2016, following
what was then the warmest and wettest UK December since records began in
1910.

Snowdrops, Daffodils, Celandines and Butterbur had been blooming
around Christmas, all species that are early-flowering but far in advance
of the norm. More strange still were blossoms showing around my home
river valley on spring- and summer-flowering Common Hogweed, Herb
Robert, Valerian, Primrose, Daisy, White Dead-nettle, Yarrow, Dandelion,
Red Dead-nettle, Germander Speedwell, Ivy-leaved Toadflax, Bitter Cress,
Perennial Sow-thistle and Groundsel... even Hawthorn, the 'May tree' so
named for the normal month of its flowering. Blue Tits were also bustling in

and out of our nest box, well in advance of the glut of spring insects vital for the nutrition of any chicks that they might rear.

Moving into the second week of January, we were promised cooler weather. However, such is the unpredictability of the jet stream and ensuing weather patterns that we were, and remain, as likely to see the return of record-breaking mild conditions as an excoriating freeze.

The study of plant and animal life cycle events is known as phenology. Long-term phenological records – such as the emergence of leaves and flowers, the first flight of butterflies, the first call of the Common Cuckoo and the reappearance of Swallows and House Martins – all highlight that the world around us is changing. Our own day-to-day observations – how late leaves now stay on the trees, how grass grows all year round, unseasonal flowerings – confirm we are living in a time of profound change.

This matters because the myriad interconnections within nature are elaborately co-evolved, such that the seeds and berries of plants feed overwintering birds and mammals, emerging aquatic insects feed juvenile fish, post-hibernation bats and summer-migrant birds, flooding cycles enable spawning fish to access marginal wetlands, the nectar of flowers feeds insects of the same season to mutual advantage and the nourishment of linked food chains, and so on and on. Break the timings and nature, though adaptive, is less resilient.

This is of far deeper concern than mere altruism about wildlife. In rural Indian and African regions where much of my professional life revolves, people live close to ecosystems. Their wellbeing – physical, economic and spiritual – is tied umbilically to the productivity of soils and forests, fisheries and rangelands, returning migratory species, the emergence of seasonal fruits and other natural produce, and the timing and quality of water flows.

This connection with natural processes is something we have lost sight of in the developed world, historic trading advantages enabling us to access global productivity via a range of supermarkets and online sources. But, in a world of fast-changing geopolitics, population and climatic instability, the reality is that we are in no way immune from the cold winds of disrupted phenology. Increasingly, we pay for it through mounting flood risk, storm damage and other extreme weather, erosion of productive soils, declining natural beauty, lost recreational opportunity and the costs of resources of all kinds.

This is why global-scale agreements on management and restoration of the climate, marine environment and land matter to all of us, locally and personally. We may enjoy a warm winter from the perspective of reduced heating bills and unexpected flowers greeting us as we walk by the river, but these are also wake-up calls about our responsibility for the future.

Our individual actions and influences, responding as best we can to what we observe around us, all have a bearing on the direction that society will take as we face unprecedented challenges in securing a stable and rich future for all... including the life-affirming and life-sustaining wildlife of the river valley.

SPARE THE DREDGER!

I T JUST TAKES a bit of flooding for half the population to become hydro-
logical and hydrogeomorphological experts! Rash, opportunist political
point-scoring adds to this cacophony, scientific realities and reasoned decision-
making its net casualties.

A significant objective reality is that we live within a changing climate in
which environmental variability, including drought and flood vulnerability, is
becoming more extreme. Another reality is our foolhardy and incautious habit
of building houses, factories and supermarkets as well as transport and other
infrastructure on floodplains. The clue is in the name: FLOODplain. Add
to this the embankment or drainage of low-lying land for farming purposes,

and we leave water nowhere to be stored to eke out flows in dry weather or to retain floodwater during intense rainfall.

We have also sealed soil surfaces through built infrastructure as well as rural land-use practices compacting surface soils, massively reducing the landscape's permeability and sponge-like properties. Unable to infiltrate, water instead rushes overland, exacerbating erosion and flood risk, with less water also stored within landscapes as a reservoir to tide us through drier months. Flooding, erosion and drought impacts are exacerbated as a tightly linked package through undermining natural processes of great public benefit.

So, as claimed by many politicians and the blame-hungry media, will dredging solve all our ills?

Tens or hundreds of square miles of impermeable catchment area and loss of floodplain upstream substantially magnify flood risk at 'bottlenecks' in river systems. Dredging will make virtually no difference, given massive peak flows. If upstream dredging occurs, it only accelerates surges of floodwater reaching 'pinch points' further downstream, and channel straightening reduces catchment storage by shortening the functional length of river systems, serving only to accelerate their flows. Deepened channels of raging floodwater are a major hazard, let alone an eyesore.

Consequently, if ill-informed political diktat precipitates deep dredging and river-straightening, we'd simply be repeating the errors and substantial associated costs of mass post-War land drainage. Declines in wildlife and natural fishery wealth, as well as soil loss and vulnerability to urban flooding, are all indicative of the scale of degradation of natural riverine processes with their myriad associated, substantially unrecognised costs. And that's before we think about where to put all that dredged spoil!

So, let's apply a bit of nature-based common sense and just stop building on floodplains. Rivers are far more than simple pipes for ridding storm water, as we may have historically treated them. They are complex, living systems interconnected with terrestrial ecosystems. Eliminate their natural functions and bad outcomes are guaranteed, not only for housing planned on land prone routinely to flood thigh-deep but also for downstream communities.

Let's also resist political rhetoric trivialising the dredging/river management debate as some sort of 'bunny-hugging versus development' dichotomy. Nature is far more than an expendable 'nice-to-have'. Nature's forms, functions and cycles store, slow and purify water, maintain soil fertility and prevent its loss, provide characteristic landscapes, sustain viable fisheries and pleasant places, cleanse the air, stabilise the climate and perform many other essential services besides. Development degrading natural functions on floodplains and elsewhere is likely to represent substantial net social costs and liabilities, offset against any short-term gains.

Let's then instead be smart and plan strategically to retain this natural value, for example in where we place intensive developments and farming activities. As, if we degrade nature's 'sponge effect' and other functions storing and cleansing water also serving many other beneficial outcomes, overall consequences can only be bad in the longer term.

A key lesson from seasonally recurring flooding is that we and the natural world are deeply, irrevocably interconnected; the sooner we recognise and factor that into our plans, the richer and less risky a future we will build for ourselves.

FEBRUARY

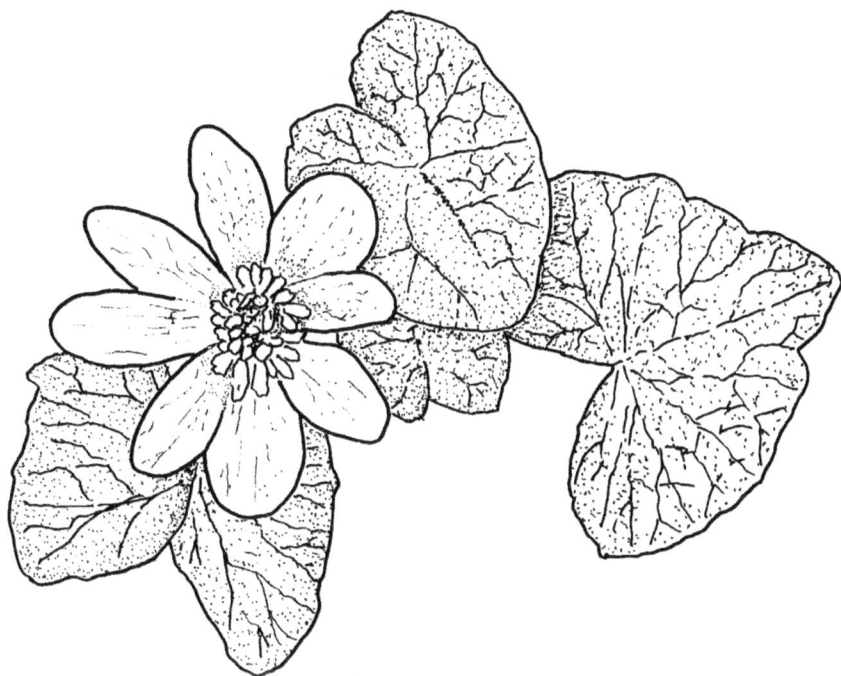

GRIDIRONS

W ITH THE LOW sun's angle, cropped turf and high water table at this time of year, patterns of channels, ridges and furrows become evident on areas of some floodplains mainly across southern Britain. With heavy rains, depressions may fill to trace a clearly man-made 'herringbone' of channels. What are these strange 'gridirons', grey-silvered where water reflects overcast skies contrasting with the green sward?

Thomas Hardy spoke of 'gridirons' in *Tess of the D'Urbervilles*, describing managed floodplains in his beloved home landscape in Dorset. Quite distinct from mere flooded fields, these managed 'water meadows' are the brilliant innovations of agricultural pioneers from the late 16th Century.

The classic form of a water meadow is a riparian floodplain engineered into ridges and furrows. In late winter and early spring, water meadows are 'floated' (or 'drowned') by diverting flows from the river with a small weir and control sluices, directing it through a series of 'floating channels' (or 'mains'), the finest of which run along the tops of the ridges, where it overtops to trickle down the sloping 'panes' into 'drain' channels in the furrows. Drains may return water to the river, or form 'head mains' feeding further water meadows downstream. The knack was to bring water 'on at a trot and off at a gallop', maintaining continuous flows down the panes with no ponding, waterlogging or deoxygenation.

This fine balance was skilled and labour-intensive, particularly where cascades of water meadows required careful manipulation to also ensure sufficient river flows for mills and navigation. These skilled artisans were known as 'Drowners', floating the meadows and repairing them in later autumn and early winter ready for the coming year. Drowners were respected members of farming communities. You didn't want to upset one if you wanted a reliable flow of water, particularly when rivers were flowing 'good and thick' bearing rich silt to fertilise the meadow.

Ingenious, but why?

In pre-industrial times, stock animals provided traction, food, wool, skins and fertiliser, but their numbers were limited by the 'hungry gap' between depletion of hay from the previous summer and the emergence of fresh grazing. Stock in excess of feed spelled catastrophe, financially and worse.

The genius of the water meadow system was not merely bringing water and nutrients from the river to land, but above all utilising the water's warmth to promote sward growth whilst ensuring it stayed well oxygenated. Grass on the panes grew prolifically, even in icy air, breaking the 'hungry gap'.

Rowland Vaughan is credited with innovating water meadows, building the first system in the Golden Valley of Herefordshire in the early 1580s. So significant was the innovation that virtually every floodplain that was suitable (and a few that weren't) was converted across southern England and many places beyond. The technology itself was uniquely British.

Water meadows declined with industrialisation of agriculture, costs and availability of labour during the Industrial Revolution, and growing import markets. The last ones on the Bristol Avon ceased operation in the 1960s. Relic systems are, however, common across Wessex, particularly adjacent to chalk rivers, also occurring elsewhere across southern England, Norfolk, Derbyshire and in valleys around Cirencester and the upper Bristol Avon. Only some half-a-dozen water meadows are actively worked today; a fascinating spectacle when steaming and lush with tall grass on a cold, frosty morning!

One day, we'll need this traditional wisdom again, as the cost, availability and downstream consequences of current high inputs of petrochemical energy and agrochemicals in contemporary intensive farming systems create increasing constraints. We have much to learn from the traditional wisdoms underpinning these often overlooked relics in our contemporary riverine landscapes.

WHAT'S A FISH?

I T'S EXCITING TO spot fish in the river. We also encounter fish cooked in batter and as a calming presence in dentists' waiting rooms. Thereafter, perhaps we give fish little second thought.

Fish are defined as limbless, aquatic cold-blooded vertebrates with gills and fins. However, they are more than that.

Fish are enjoyed for recreational purposes through angling, aquaria and ponds, or 'fish twitching'. The value of angling to the UK runs into £ billions, and angling activities also promote social inclusion. Ornamental fish are prized in Japanese culture where prices and possession of the finest koi carp are closely guarded secrets, though one specimen was reportedly bought for a staggering $US2.2 million. The global value of trade in ornamental fish exceeds US$7 billion annually.

We may enjoy eating fish, supporting large markets for cookery programmes, books and restaurants. However, fish are the primary protein source for approximately 1 billion people. Global fish production exceeds poultry, beef or pork. Fishing, fish processing and sales are major contributors to employment worldwide adding $US274 billion to global GDP.

We put fish to diverse other uses including as fertiliser, stock animal feed, ornamental resources and oil extraction. (The eulachon from the Pacific coast contains so much fat that it can be strung and burned as a candle). The sharp, tough scales of Amazonia's Arapaima (*Arapaima* species) were traditionally used as arrowheads, and the enormous scales of India's Mahseer fishes (*Tor* species) as dinner plates or decoration.

Some fish regulate diseases, particularly controlling snails, water fleas, mosquito larvae and other vectors spreading serious conditions such as Malaria, Bilharzia, River Blindness and Guinea Worm.

Fish also indicate the health of the water environment, their needs informing quality standards used in management that also protects our many uses of water. Several US cities hold fish in intakes to municipal water supplies to counter terrorism, particularly since 9/11, fish behaviour providing early warning of contamination since their responses are more sensitive and immediate than laboratory apparatus.

Fish have diverse spiritual meanings across the world, from the Christian symbol of the Ichthus to the first Avatar of Vishnu taking the form of the fish Matsya in the Hindu tradition, and the catfish Namazu that causes earthquakes in Japan but is restrained with a stone by the god Kashima.

Fish stimulate art and entertainment, such as Henry Williamson's *Salar the Salmon*, Franz Schubert's *Die Forelle*, many popular songs, paintings of charismatic species, a wide library of fishy books, and frequent fishy themes on TV programmes such as BBC's *Springwatch* and *Planet Earth*.

Fish also mobilise public activism around conservation projects, for example their roles in the founding and management, campaigning and educational activities of the UK's Rivers Trust NGO (non-governmental organisations) network.

Many freshwater fish species are also of conservation concern. Freshwater habitats are amongst the most threatened ecosystems globally. 38% of Europe's freshwater fish species are threatened with extinction with a further 12 already extinct, and approximately 20% of the world's 10,000 freshwater fish species are listed as threatened, endangered or extinct. Our concern for fish should be far more than altruistic, as this decline indicates a commensurate reduction in the capacities of ecosystems to support our needs.

So fish are far more than something enjoyed in batter or observed from a river bridge. The contributions that fish and the aquatic ecosystems of which they are a part make to our continuing health, wealth, quality of life and future security are as diverse as they are substantial.

What is a fish? Their meanings are as diverse as the span of human perceptions and value systems.

RETURN OF THE OTTER

MANY PEOPLE HAVEN'T seen a wild Otter. Yet, from the later 1990s, these charismatic mammals have been an increasing presence across all of Britain's river valleys.

The Eurasian Otter (*Lutra lutra*) was formerly widespread throughout Britain until innovation of novel, persistent, wide-spectrum pesticides, largely for agricultural intensification following the Second World War, resulted in accumulation of problematic chemicals in the tissues of top predators. Otters were particularly vulnerable, numbers crashing to a nadir in the 1980s leaving relic populations in the less agriculturally intense 'Celtic fringe': far south-west England, west Wales, and north and west Scotland.

Dawning recognition of dangers inherent in incautious use of persistent pesticides instigated progressive phase-out and control of many substances. Subsequently, we've witnessed recovery of Buzzards, Kestrels, various owl species and other predators. Recovery of British Otters since the 1990s has followed at a slower, albeit predicted pace.

Otter signs – sightings, spraints (droppings used as territorial markers), paw prints, rolling sites and trampled trackways inside river meanders – became increasingly common as the species spread southwards and eastwards. Today, Otter signs occur in every county, with populations established in many.

Adjacent to recovering populations in Somerset and the Severn, the Bristol Avon was recognised as ripe for re-colonisation in the early-1990s. An artificial holt (Otter breeding den) was built near my home in North Wiltshire. However, like every other artificial holt that I know, it proved popular with Badgers and Foxes but never with Otters! But Otters have nevertheless returned.

The first unambiguous Otter signs I saw on my home river were in the mid-1990s. My first actual sighting was in the early 2000s of a very big dog Otter, big enough to nearly mistake for a badger as it approached at dusk. I've subsequently seen many smaller female Otters, some almost within touching distance and in full daylight, as well as other larger dog Otters that seem utterly fearless. This is partly luck, but enhanced by my propensity to sit unobtrusively by the riverside into dusk with a fishing rod.

Otters now occupy much of the Bristol Avon, my home river from which they were absent for many years. They are a constant if largely nocturnal presence around our villages. Within a short walk from my back door, I could show you various sprainting sites (places where characteristic droppings, sweet-smelling and containing small fish bones, mark Otter territories). So too many other southern and eastern English rivers. You could get lucky with a sighting if you sat quietly into dusk.

During the recovery phase of the 1990s and early 2000s, road kills accounted for most Otter mortality. Today, Otter territories – a dog Otter may control ten or more miles of river spanning the territories of four or more female Otters – are fully occupied in many recovered catchments. Wounds inflicted in fights between these fiercely territorial creatures are believed now to be the main contributor to mortality.

The Otter's return isn't uniformly welcomed. Some quarters of the angling press vilify the Otter for eating fish. The demise (a 95% loss over a decade) of the European Eel – formerly a staple of the Otter – places greater pressure on other fish species. Yet predators of all kinds are entirely natural elements of intricate ecological balances. I and at least some other angling writers regularly remind readers that Otter populations boomed throughout former perceived 'golden ages' of angling and fish stocks. A healthy river sustains thriving stocks of all species – prey and predator alike – so focussing on the vitality of river ecosystems is the overriding priority, rather than demonising a single perceived villain, particularly a territorial species so ruthlessly efficient at controlling its own numbers!

Given a choice between an environment too toxic for its top predators or, alternatively, their resurgence, I know unambiguously where I stand. The resurgence of our native Otter, in the face of the myriad other pressures on our river and future, is then surely very welcome indeed!

HUMBLE BEES

O N WARM, HIGH pressure days in late February, the first bumblebees
can often be seen taking to the wing, these bulbous and furry bundles
foraging amongst the vegetation by the river and hedgerows.

Or rather, humblebees, for that was how they were known by Charles
Darwin and in his era.

The term bumblebee is a later renaming. 'Humble' referred not
to perceived lowly worth but simply because, as they fly, they hum.
Authoritative texts from the second decade of the twentieth century were
firmly rooted in the term 'humblebee', some acknowledging 'bumblebee' as a
minor nickname. However, Beatrix Potter – incidentally a leading mycologist
(fungal scientist) in her lifetime which many people do not realise – published
the Tale of Mrs Tittlemouse in 1910, her titular rodent troubled by squatters
making mossy nests in her back yard and prime amongst them being one
Babbitty Bumble. Another theory about the rise of the name 'bumblebee' is
that, with the emergence of the science and wider appreciation of aeronautics
in the inter-War era, there emerged a flawed theory that it was impossible for
the tubby, short-winged bumblebee to fly. So the idea of these furry creatures
bumbling inefficiently from blossom to blossom rather took hold, somewhat in

defiance of evolutionary reality, such that the original term humblebee had all but vanished by the late 1950s.

Globally, over 250 species of bumblebee are known. Of the 250 bee species in the British Isles, 24 are bumblebees characterised by round bodies covered in soft hair giving them a fuzzy appearance, coloured in contrasting bands as a warning colour advertising to would-be predators that they are capable of stinging. Like honeybees, bumblebees feed on nectar, using their long hairy tongues to lap it up and gathering it to store in their nests, as well as bringing pollen back to feed their young. For this reason, bumblebees are important agricultural pollinators, so their decline across the northern hemisphere through habitat loss, agricultural mechanisation and pesticides is a major cause for concern. Bumblebee nests are generally small, comprising as few as 50 individuals and a single queen.

Amazingly, there is a group of 'cuckoo bumblebees', six species of which are found in the UK. Cuckoo bumblebees lack a queen but, like the bird from which they derive their name, the female enters the nest of a true bumblebee, often hiding in nest debris for some time before killing the social bumblebee queen and laying her own eggs in the nest for worker bumblebees to unknowingly raise. Emerging cuckoo bumblebees leave the nest to mate, before the females go into hibernation.

Bumblebees have been of use and inspiration to people throughout history. Yes, as important workers pollinating crops and keeping the wheel of nature turning. But also inspiring the Russian composer Nikolai Rimsky-Korsakov to write his orchestral interlude *Flight of the Bumblebee* in around 1900. This music was in turn picked up by Walt Disney as backing to animation of a bumblebee in an early version of the 1940 musical movie *Fantasia*.

Many references to the bumblebee also appear in literature and art, from Emily Dickinson's *The Bumble-Bee's Religion* (1881), through many treatises, poems, watercolours, and of course Beatrix Potter's Babbity Bumble. The surname 'Dumbledore' in the Harry Potter series was also an ancient name for the bumblebee, and one that author J.K. Rowling has said that she felt suited the often ponderous, music-loving headmaster.

For me, the sight and often soporific hum of humblebees at work gathering nectar and pollen is heart-warming, never more so during those pioneering, early-spring days when warmth slowly seeps back into the winter-wracked riverscape and its wondrous kaleidoscope of living things.

THE NATURE OF NATURE

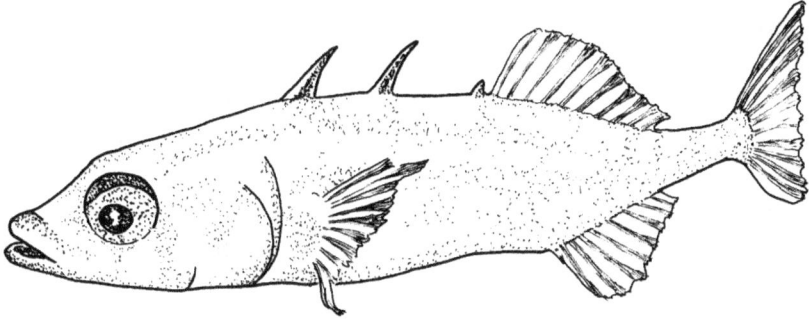

Nature broadcasting is a media evergreen.
Polar bears brave the ravages of climate change in the Arctic, great herds of wildebeest on the East African savannah are hunted by lions and ambushed by crocodiles, salmon make prodigious leaps to overcome weirs and other barriers driven on by the urgency of reaching natal spawning grounds, and so the images roll on.

Closer to home, in more moderate climates and everyday settings, the zig-zag mating dance of male sticklebacks, 'boxing' hares or a blinking row of barn owl chicks are popular images.

These visions are compelling; warming even.

Other images, such as the sheer awfulness of a turtle strangled by marine plastic litter of our making, are motivating and can become powerful stimuli of shifts in societal mind sets. Above all, these natural images reconnect us to wildernesses and wildness expunged as much by the clamour for our attention of pervasive media as by the sprawl of concrete and asphalt. But they can also perpetuate a cognitive deception.

That deception is that nature is 'out there'; something remote from ourselves, to cherish altruistically and enjoy sporadically and vicariously. Even the very word 'environment' is generally defined and understood as that which surrounds us; something there, but essentially something other than us.

The awareness that we have lost is that we ARE nature, inseparably connected with nature's greater cycles of which all living and non-living components, including ourselves, are one whole interactive system. We breathe, drink and eat nature, and reciprocally nature reprocesses as a feedstock our bodily waste gases, liquids and solids into renewed resources. The energy powering every cell in our bodies 24/7 arrived as photons from the sun, captured though the alchemy of photosynthesis into the bonds of complex molecules that reach us and leave us again through circuitous natural cycles in which many and diverse life forms play pivotal roles.

Our industries and municipalities are as much metabolic entities as we biological human beings, feeding on flows of natural fibre, minerals, energy and other of nature's essential resources, with nature then re-assimilating their diverse excretions as best it is capable.

Nature does not withhold support for the diverse biophysical, spiritual, aesthetic and commercial uses that we make of it, though through our weight of numbers and ill-thought uses and abuses of its resources we may compromise the limits of natural processes to nourish and maintain our health, wealth and wellbeing into the future.

Not until we understand the nature of nature fully can we reflect as fully on the lifestyle habitats and expectations with which we have grown up, doing so generally in a dangerously unquestioning manner. Not until we see nature in the fuel in our vehicles and their emissions, and the food in our shopping baskets and the many production, processing and transport processes that put it there, can we truly perceive what living in synergy with nature's unstintingly supportive ecosystems really means.

Only then can we find the insight and wisdom necessary to begin to make serious inroads into the lifestyle revisions that are necessary as our duty, as elements of nature gifted with the intelligence to innovate but also now with the knowledge and foresight to do so in ways that are harmonious with the wonders of this most marvellous natural world that is both our inheritance and our legacy.

Enjoy and be inspired by nature, in the wild and on the screen, for it is marvellous and life-affirming. But, above all, we have also to discover nature within ourselves and as an integral element of every facet of our everyday lives.

MARCH

MARCH MAGIC!

I 'VE OFTEN FOUND that the season for which people feel the deepest affection corresponds with that of their birth. Doubtless, there are myriad reasons for this. But it is certainly the case for me, a child of the Ides of March (infamous throughout history including the date of Julius Caesar's sticky demise), though I also find mystery and inspiration in every season.

As March unfolds, often imperceptibly slowly yet inexorably around us, the riverscape morphs from winter's muted hues into soft greenery. And, whilst the froth of Blackthorn blossom echoes the white flush of hoar frosts still visited upon hedgerows not infrequently in the early weeks, bursting leaf buds of Hawthorn and various willows flush the scrub with pale green vibrancy towards month's end.

One day, a bumblebee emerges from winter drowse, its rotund body plying the air on inconceivably small wings. Then, a hoverfly may appear, sunning itself on a leaf before seeking out mates and water in which to lay eggs. Soon, queen wasps burst out from the papery tombs of last summer's otherwise dead nests, pioneering matriarchs fanning out across the countryside to found a new season's empire. Queen Hornets too can be seen, far scarcer and larger insects with a baritone drone in flight yet a gentler disposition and more amber hue than the wasp's yellow, as they quarter the waking landscape for a sheltered nook in which to establish a new colony.

One bright day, a Small Tortoiseshell butterfly may slough off its overwintering slumber in a dead tree, log pile or outbuilding, finding a warm niche in bark, stone or a foot-worn path on which to spread gaudy wings to greet and capture warmth from the strengthening sunshine, before then taking flight. Perhaps a Peacock butterfly too may take to the cool early spring air, all velvet black on their wings' undersides yet stunningly eyed on their upper faces.

Kingfishers pair above the cold, green water in their uneasy mating truce. Moorhens fan out from communal harmony on larger rivers and lakes to establish and defend territories in wet pockets across the broader landscape. In river margins, where adventitious dark green and purple shoots of fresh Reed Canary Grass pierce the mud and straw of last-year's reed beds, Mallards pair and seek out nesting sites, serenaded by spring songs from countless smaller birds in the surrounding vegetation.

Underfoot, Celandine flowers will have been peaking from river banks and pockets of moist earth in small clumps for a month or possibly more, but come into profuse fullness as March unfurls. Their hot yellow is complemented as the month progresses by the cooler tone of Primrose flowers opening to greet the rising season. Dusty yellow cascades of 'lamb's tails' droop lush from woody Sallow twigs and, towards the month's latter half, the cool air is splashed by the livid sulphur of male Brimstone butterflies (*Gonepteryx rhamni*) as they burst out from overwintering cocoons on spring-fresh wings in advance of the later-emerging, paler female insects.

River flies too start to emerge: up-wing, caddis and midge. Common Pipistrelles (*Pipistrellus pipistrellus*), Daubenton's Bat (*Myotis daubentonii*) and other species of bat wake and take wing, initially singly then in greater numbers, to hawk the river at dusk to replenish themselves on this emerging insect feast after their winter-long fast.

March is a time of awakening, of the unleashing of energies held at bay by the dark, cool grip of winter. It is a time of release, of a joyous form of madness... you may even spot a Hare of two 'madly' boxing in courtship battles on the riverside meadows!

LOW-FLYING MICE

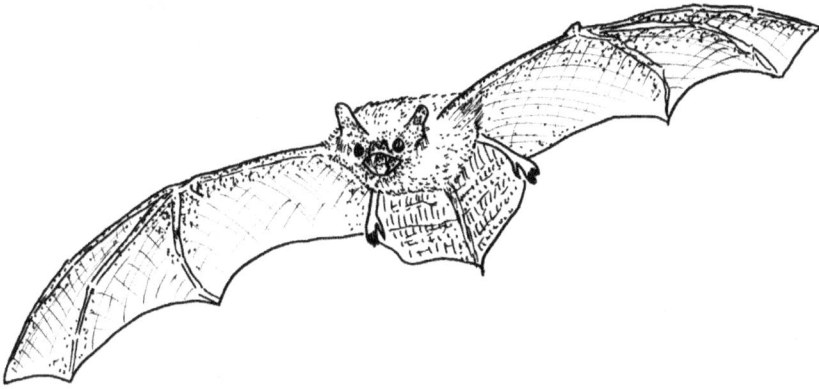

D IE *FLEDERMAUS* – the Flying Mouse – is a well-known operetta by Johann Strauss II, but also the German word for 'Bat'. German is kinder to the bat than the French *Chauve-suris*, or 'Bald Mouse'. 'Flying Mouse' is not a bad descriptor of all but the bulkiest fruit bats, though bats comprise a discrete and large pan-global group – the only mammals with true flight though others can glide – distinct from mice and other rodents.

These chiroptocentric (bat-centred) musings are prompted by the re-emergence of bats over the river after winter dormancy. Many British species of bat truly hibernate whilst some, such as the common and widely distributed Common Pipistrelle (*Pipistrellus pipistrellus*), can wake on milder winter evenings to emerge for a quick snack of insects, also encouraged to take to the air, before resuming semi-hibernation.

In early springtime though, bats like many other living things on our Isles, appear initially singly then progressively in greater numbers and diversity to hawk for dusk-flying insects over open water surfaces, lanes bordered by hedgerows, woodland rides and fringes, and gardens. They are a signal of warmer times, of dusk encroaching, and of nature's profusion and diversity.

But the poor old bats suffer an undeserved 'bad press'. Chiroptophobia – 'fear of bats' in Greek – is a common human condition. Association with Dracula is melodramatic, when in reality only three South American species of vampire bat feed on blood, only one of these doing so primarily on mammals (occasionally humans) and the other two from birds. Then there is the fear of bats carrying rabies: in fact, a vanishingly small proportion of the few, remotely occurring blood-eating bats do carry rabies but, as rabid bats are non-aggressive and die quickly, the chances of the disease passing to humans is about as likely as getting trampled by a unicorn. The fear of bats getting tangled in people's hair is also not uncommon, when in reality bats perceive us very clearly even if we can't see them in the gloom. Their acute faculties famously include echolocation: sensing objects around themselves from the echoes of high-pitched sound waves, generally many octaves beyond the acuity of human hearing, emitted from their mouths. The reality is that, due to this precision locational sense, bats are as likely to get tangled in your hair as are swallows, blackbirds, golden eagles or low-flying dragons.

So why should we learn to love bats just a little more? Well, apart from being fascinating and diverse lifestyles – there are seventeen species of bat in the UK alone – bats do amazing things beyond the miracle of echolocation. As predators of flying insects, bats play roles in controlling some bugs that might otherwise become pests and others that can carry diseases. For example, the Pipistrelle, widely distributed across Europe, North Africa and South West Asia, may be a tiny mammal with a body length of between 1¼ and 1¾ inches from head to tail, but a single adult can consume 3,000 mosquitoes during a single night. Elsewhere around the world, various different predominantly fruit-eating bats serve as pollinators, maintaining biodiversity and playing important roles in production of crops including Century Plants (Agave) from Central American that are used in the production of tequila.

Across Britain, as indeed across Eurasia as far east as Japan, the robustly built Daubenton's Bat (*Myotis daubentonii*) has a close affinity with rivers and lakes, and is consequently often known as the 'water bat'. As the activity of Common Pipistrelles and Daubenton's, Long-eared, Greater and Lesser Horseshoe and other bat species intensifies over and around the river with the rise of spring, we all have the chance to notice and, I hope, appreciate them that little bit more.

THE MUNDELLA
LEGACY

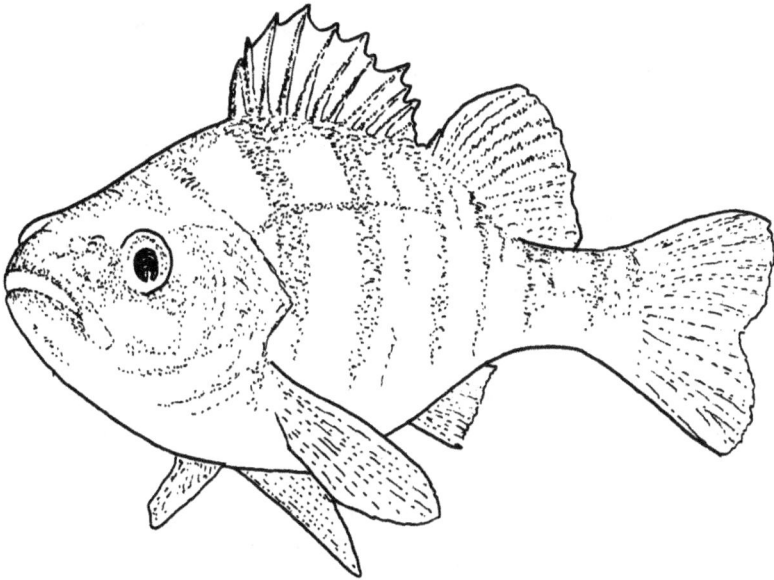

FISH ARE THE primary protein source for about one-fifth of the global
human population, and for a far greater proportion in many countries.
River and lake fisheries support a major proportion of this need. So it was
until comparatively recently in the UK, and so it remains across much of
continental Europe. Common Carp (*Cyprinus carpio*), for example, are
traditionally eaten at Christmas in Hungary and other eastern European
countries, and most French anglers tend to take home even the smallest of
fishes that they catch.

Towards the latter half of the nineteenth century, growing concerns
about potential depletion of freshwater fish populations led Anthony John
Mundella to petition for and drive through legislation relating to their
protection.

Who was Mundella? Actually, he was an impressive figure, albeit
little known today. A.J. Mundella was born in Leicester in March 1825,
the son of Italian refugees, rising from his station as a hosiery manufacturer
to become a prominent reformer and Liberal Party politician. Mundella

was first asked to stand for parliament to defend the interests of labour in the wake of the Sheffield Outrages, a civil uprising by working classes upon whom were inflicted the worst demeaning and health-threatening conditions of the Industrial Revolution. Mundella sat in the House of Commons from 1868 until his death in 1897, including two stints as President of the Board of Trade. During his time in the House, Mundella was an active champion of compulsory education in England, a driving force behind the Elementary Education Act of 1870 and also the educational code of 1882 that became known as the 'Mundella Code'. He was a major force behind the Factory Act of 1875, establishing a ten-hour day for women and children in textile factories, and the Conspiracy Act that removed certain restrictions on trade unions. Mundella was also a driving force behind many more pieces of socially progressive and animal health legislation, leaving a significant mark on the fabric of Great Britain that persists to this day.

Mundella was also concerned with the wellbeing of our freshwater fish stocks. Prompted by a consortium of 7,000 or so anglers in his constituency of Sheffield, Mundella drove through proposals "...which will permit of freshwater fish completing the procreation of their species in peace and quiet". Vociferous debates ensued about the time period this should cover, noting both the different spawning times of different coarse fish species ('game' species such as salmon and trout spawn in the winter and so are now covered by different closed seasons), and also considerable variation according inter-annual and geographic factors. But, to cut a long and acrimonious debate short, the consensual period spanned the middle of March to the middle of June. This was a compromise, splitting the difference between a Sheffield proposal of March to May and a London counter-proposal of April to June, forming the basis for the coarse fishing closed season from 15th March to 15th June (inclusive) enshrined in the Freshwater Fisheries Act of 1878 (the 'Mundella Act') and rolled forward on rivers to this day across England and Wales.

Every year, there are representations – mainly economic – for the river coarse fishing closed season to be removed. (The battle was lost in the 1990s on retaining the closed season on still waters, primarily for economic reasons.) After all, British recreational coarse anglers today no longer take coarse fish for the table. However, I side strongly with the legacy of Mundella: whilst a fixed 93-day span may not cover all species every year in all corners of the country, the basic tenet that coarse fishes deserve their period of undisturbed procreation when they are at their most vulnerable is one I wholeheartedly support.

HERE BE
PTERODACTYLS!

WHEN OUR DAUGHTER Daisy was little, she came night fishing with me a couple of times. With her tucked up safely in a sleeping bag under a brolly behind my chair, we'd chatter and watch the night life until sleep took us.

One still, overcast night, a hoarse cry suddenly ripped the silence right above us. A small hand reached out for mine in the darkness. *"Are you scared?"* I asked. *"No"* came the reply, then *"Well maybe a bit!"*

I just caught a silhouette wheeling away between the trees before vanishing into the gloom. Surprised as us, the creature had emitted its disgruntled cackle when air-braking on broad wings, spanning some 2 metres, on suddenly finding strange bipeds blocking its nocturnal landing platform.

In the dark, the vocal protest and profile of the Grey Heron (*Ardea cinerea*) were those of a pterodactyl, an impression deepened when so sudden and unexpected. But the sight of a Grey Heron paddling through the sky in broad daylight, head characteristically tucked back and legs extended behind, still resembles a long-extinct flying reptile. Mercifully for us, its diet comprises fish, amphibians and occasional small mammals captured in or near water.

By March, sometimes February in warm years, Grey Herons start nesting. They congregate from across broad landscapes just for this purpose and until the youngsters fledge, gathering in traditional heronries in the tops of tall trees varying from small congregations to those containing over a hundred birds. Some heronries endure for centuries, renewed annually with twigs and branches. Both parent birds brood their 3-5 eggs, taking turns to search for food, returning to the nest with fish for the ever-hungry, fast-growing young once they hatch. Later, pair bonds break up and the juvenile birds too – characterised by less developed head feathers and other plumage – spread out over the countryside and by urban waters.

The Grey Heron is one of Britain's tallest birds, though the Mute Swan (*Cygnus olor*) is heavier and has a wider wingspan. Other species of heron occur in the UK. Three species of egret, all white, have become established, the most widespread being the Little Egret (*Egretta garzetta*) now widely seen across southern England though formerly rare or absent. Cheekily perhaps, egrets often nest in the lower boughs of heronries, benefitting from the protection of their bigger cousins. Sometimes, the Purple Heron (*Ardea purpurea*) arrives as a vagrant. Our rarest heron is the scarce and shy Bittern (*Botaurus stellaris*), a once-common but now threatened wetland bird most frequently now found in the east of England but visiting some scattered large wetland areas further to the west, such the Cotswold Water Park on the Gloucestershire/Wiltshire border.

Most heronries are in undisturbed locations, often on private land, as the birds are readily disturbed. Heronries get seriously smelly as the nesting season progresses, copious liquefied guano excreted in white streams by parent and juvenile birds, painting the trees and forest floor and not uncommonly killing some trees under the onslaught of noxious, fishy waste.

Some years back, I spent time photographing Grey Herons for a book. This posed two challenges. The first was getting close enough to these notoriously flighty birds, overcome by visiting greener waterside areas of cities where the birds are so habituated that you can walk almost right up to them. The second challenge was harder: trying to get a picture of one looking anything other than bored, as Grey Herons spend much of their time inert either resting or waiting for prey to ambush with a quick thrust of their spear-like beaks.

To some, this bird is the 'Grey Fisher', to others 'Old Nog or 'The Grumpy Old Man of the River'. To me, they are more like the pterodactyl's long-lost cousin!

TURN! TURN! TURN!

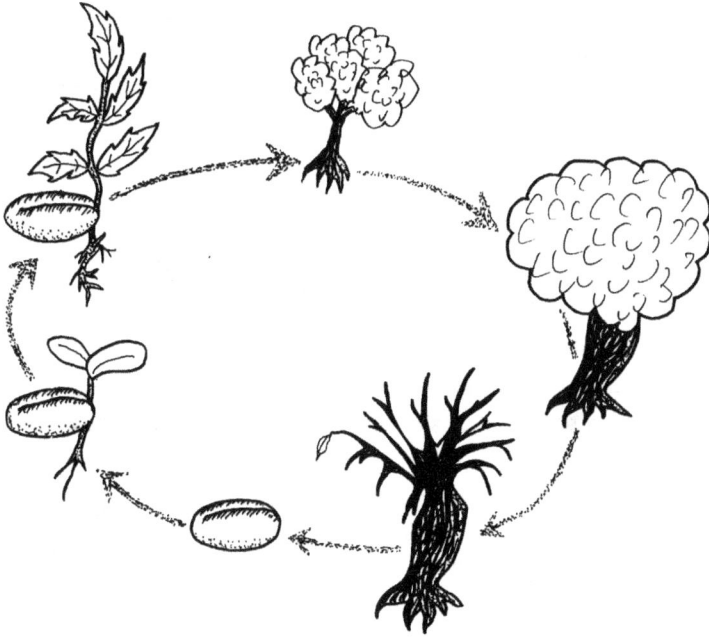

THE CHAPTER TITLE may be familiar to readers of a certain age, as it is the name of an international hit song in 1965 by American folk rock group The Byrds. The song itself was actually written in the late 1950s by the American folk singer and social activist Pete Seeger.

The song is a favourite of mine, The Byrds version still an evergreen on the radio, resonant not merely for its musicality but for what it has to say.

In fact, all of the lyrics except the song's title, repeated throughout the song, derive from the King James Version (1611) of The Bible (Ecclesiastes 3:1-8). We can repeat these words here without fear of copyright infringement (but ironically not so the words of the song adopting them!)

> To every thing there is a season, and a time to every purpose under the
> heaven:
> A time to be born, and a time to die; a time to plant, a time to reap that
> which is planted;
> A time to kill, and a time to heal; a time to break down, and a time to

build up;

A time to weep, and a time to laugh; a time to mourn, and a time to dance;

A time to cast away stones, and a time to gather stones together;

A time to embrace, and a time to refrain from embracing;

A time to get, and a time to lose; a time to keep, and a time to cast away;

A time to rend, and a time to sew; a time to keep silence, and a time to
   speak;

A time to love, and a time to hate; a time of war, and a time of peace.

The song has meaning for many people, regardless of its derivation. It speaks of the transience of all things. It is a source of solace in times that are hard, as also of humility in times of good fortune.

Above all, it is recognition of seasons in all things, natural and human, and the inevitability of their waxing and waning.

Rivers and their diverse and abundant life are an ultimate expression of nature's cycles, constantly repeating but in no dull, monotonous way. For everything, there is indeed a season of planting, blooming, seeding and reaping. Populations build up – of mayflies on the wing in a short fortnight, of fish over decadal cycles, of river habitats over millennia – but also break down as they progress to a new phase, assimilated in a constant regenerative cycle. Indeed, this dynamism is vital for the health and diversity of ecosystems, and their many processes from which we derive fresh water, clean air, food, spiritual and cultural enrichment, and so many other tangible and less recognised benefits.

So, whilst we experience our seasons of mourning and rejoicing, gathering and casting away, speaking and silence, conflict and resolution, the grand planetary ecosystems of which even the mightiest rivers are a microcosm do so too in a process of constant renewal.

Time by rivers can inform us of our own transience, but also of the greater progressive journey of humanity, including above all of the journey ahead to relearn how to live in harmony with planetary resources and processes upon which our future wellbeing utterly depends.

When first a hit, the song resonated with a zeitgeist of change in a post-War world of apparent rigid authority. But, like a fine wine or whisky, it has deeper notes. These notes are about the seasons inherent in all things, including rivers, their myriad life forms and all of us dependants upon them.

www.ingramcontent.com/pod-product-compliance
Lightning Source LLC
Chambersburg PA
CBHW070805280326
41934CB00012B/3067